AF445454

# Notes / Ex

# Welcome to Your
# Trailward Texas State Parks Adventure!

Trailward is your companion for exploring the trails of the Lone Star State—one path at a time. This book is designed for hikers, walkers, and explorers who want to track, plan, and remember every trail across Texas State Parks and Historic Sites.

Inside, you'll find detailed trail information, space to check off completed trails, and room to record notes from your hikes. Organized by region, Trailward helps you move park by park, trail by trail, building a personal record of where you've been and where you're headed next.

Whether you're tackling a short loop or a full-day hike, this book is here to guide your journey and capture the details that matter most along the way. Grab your boots, follow the trail ahead, and let Trailward help you leave your mark—one trail at a time.

## Join the Community!
Want to connect with other park lovers?

Join us on Instagram
@wanderstamped

Tag us & share photos, tips, trail progress, and trip recommendations with fellow adventurers across the state. We'd love to see where your journey takes you!

See you on the trails, and happy exploring!

**-The Wander Stamped Family**

**Trailward**
Texas State Parks Edition
© 2026 Wander Stamped
 All rights reserved.

No part of this publication may be reproduced, distributed, or transmitted in any form or by any means—including photocopying, recording, scanning, or other electronic or mechanical methods—without prior written permission from the publisher, except as permitted by copyright law for brief quotations in reviews or educational use.

This book is intended for personal, informational, and recreational use. While every effort has been made to ensure accuracy, trail conditions, distances, access, and park details may change. The publisher and author assume no responsibility for errors, omissions, or updates to trail information, including but not limited to hours, fees, closures, or park policies. Readers are encouraged to consult official park resources before visiting.

All Texas State Parks names, maps, and associated references are the property of the Texas Parks and Wildlife Department and are used here for informational and trail-planning purposes only. Trailward is an independently created publication and is not affiliated with, sponsored by, or endorsed by the Texas Parks and Wildlife Department.

For inquiries or permissions, contact:
**Wander Stamped**
wanderstamped@gmail.com

Printed in the United States of America
First Edition: February 2026
ISBN: 979-8-9933698-3-9

# Before You Hit the Trail

This book is designed to help you explore the trails of Texas State Parks. Each park section focuses entirely on its trail system, providing key trail information, space to check off completed trails, and room to record notes from your hikes.

Trail information and estimated hike times are based on official park data at the time of publication and may vary due to conditions, access changes, weather, or pace. For the most current information, each park section includes a QR code linking directly to the Texas Parks & Wildlife website, where you can find updated trail maps, alerts, and park notices.

At the time of publication, the following parks were not yet open to the public:
Palo Pinto Mountains State Park
Albert & Bessie Kronkosky State Natural Area
Powderhorn State Park
Bear Creek State Park

Trail pages for these parks are included so you can add information and begin tracking as trails become accessible.

At the beginning of each region, you'll find a dedicated completion space. This square is yours. Use it to place a Wander Stamped region sticker, add a park decal, attach a photo, record a milestone, or leave it blank until you've earned it. However you choose to fill it, it represents one thing: **you finished the region.**

We hope Trailward becomes your trusted companion for exploring Texas—helping you move forward one trail at a time and build a record of the paths you've traveled.

# Texas State Parks by Region

# Texas State Parks by Region

# NORTH TEXAS
## REGION

**TRAILS TO EXPLORE**
107

**PARKS INCLUDED**
12

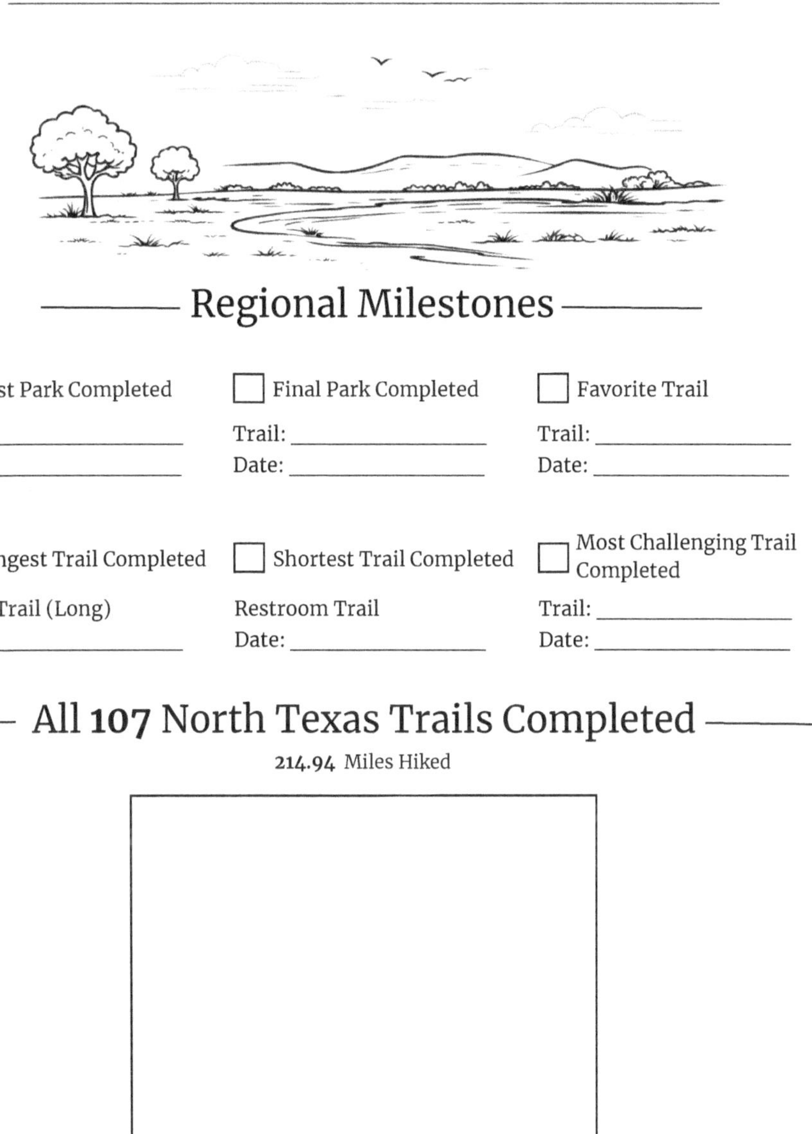

## Regional Milestones

☐ First Park Completed

Trail: _________________

Date: _________________

☐ Final Park Completed

Trail: _________________

Date: _________________

☐ Favorite Trail

Trail: _________________

Date: _________________

☐ Longest Trail Completed

Dorba Trail (Long)

Date: _________________

☐ Shortest Trail Completed

Restroom Trail

Date: _________________

☐ Most Challenging Trail Completed

Trail: _________________

Date: _________________

## All **107** North Texas Trails Completed

**214.94** Miles Hiked

Date: _________________          Total Miles Hiked: _________________

# Bonham State Park

☐ **ARMADILLO TRAIL**     1.5 mi. • Moderate          Date:__________

The path curves through dense cedar trees, offering chances to spot armadillos foraging along the forest floor.

Trail Notes: _________________________________________________

_______________________________________________________________

_______________________________________________________________

☐ **BOIS D'ARC TRAIL**     2.7 mi. • Challenging          Date:__________

Frequent elevation changes and rocky footing make this a rewarding hike. The trail passes several picnic areas and historic fireplaces built by the Civilian Conservation Corps.

Trail Notes: _________________________________________________

_______________________________________________________________

_______________________________________________________________

☐ **GNARLY ROOT TRAIL**     1.3 mi. • Moderate          Date:__________

This shaded trail winds through a hardwood forest below the dam. It's a great option for a short hike and connects to the Bois d'Arc Trail for added mileage.

Trail Notes: _________________________________________________

_______________________________________________________________

_______________________________________________________________

☐ **LAKE LOOP**     1.3 mi. • Easy          Date:__________

This mostly flat loop circles much of the lake. Quiet shoreline sections make good fishing spots, and wood ducks are often seen along the water's edge.

Trail Notes: _________________________________________________

_______________________________________________________________

_______________________________________________________________

## ⚲ Trailward Finds

☐ **CCC PUMP HOUSE**
DATE:

☐ **CCC FIREPLACE AND SEATING**
DATE:

☐ **CCC DAM**
DATE:

☐ **CCC FOOTBRIDGE**
DATE:

☐ **WILDFLOWER FIELD**
DATE:

☐ **LAKE LOOP REST STOP**
DATE:

Park Website          Trail Map

Visit the Texas Parks & Wildlife Department at tpwd.texas.gov

# Cedar Hill State Park

☐ SHORELINE TRAIL          1.0 mi. •          Easy          • 30 min.          Date:__________

This accessible trail winds along the shoreline and offers opportunities to observe wildlife along the route.

Trail Notes: ____________________________________________________

____________________________________________________

____________________________________________________

☐ PENN FARM TRAIL          0.6 mi. •          Easy          • 30 min.          Date:__________

Stroll around the historic farmstead and explore the buildings that supported the Penn family for over a century. This trail is suitable for off-road strollers.

Trail Notes: ____________________________________________________

____________________________________________________

____________________________________________________

☐ DUCK POND TRAIL          0.8 mi. •          Easy          • 35 min.          Date:__________

This short trail offers an easy walk through open fields and forested areas, with views along the edge of Duck Pond.

Trail Notes: ____________________________________________________

____________________________________________________

____________________________________________________

☐ TALALA TRAIL          2.3 mi. • Moderate •          2 hrs.          Date:__________

This trail travels through a variety of habitats and offers the park's best opportunity to view prairie restoration up close.

Trail Notes: ____________________________________________________

____________________________________________________

____________________________________________________

☐ PLUM VALLEY TRAIL          0.8 mi. • Moderate • 30 min.          Date:__________

Use this connector trail to extend your hike and reach a second overlook showcasing the unique habitat formed where the Tallgrass Blackland Prairie meets the White Rock Limestone Escarpment.

Trail Notes: ____________________________________________________

____________________________________________________

____________________________________________________

*Continued on next page*          9

# Cedar Hill State Park

☐ DORBA TRAIL (SHORT) 3.0 mi. • Challenging • Biking: 30 min. Hiking: 1.5 hrs. Date:_____________

This roughly 3-mile trail offers lake views and ample shade. Bikers travel clockwise, while hikers should go counterclockwise.

Trail Notes: _________________________________________

_________________________________________

_________________________________________

☐ DORBA TRAIL (MED.) 8.0 mi. • Challenging • Biking: 1 hr. 20min Hiking: 4 hrs. Date:_____________

This rugged 8-mile loop offers a challenging hike with steady elevation changes. Bikers travel clockwise, while hikers should go counterclockwise.

Trail Notes: _________________________________________

_________________________________________

_________________________________________

☐ DORBA TRAIL (LONG) 12.0 mi. • Challenging    Biking: 2 hrs. Hiking: 6 hrs. Date:_____________

The path curves through dense cedar trees, offering chances to spot armadillos foraging along the forest floor.

Trail Notes: _________________________________________

_________________________________________

_________________________________________

## 📍 Trailward Finds

☐ **PRAIRIE ROOTS**
DATE:

☐ **PENN FARM**
DATE:

☐ **TALALA OVERLOOK**
DATE:

☐ **PLUM VALLEY OVERLOOK**
DATE:

☐ **DUCK POND**
DATE:

Park Website    Trail Map
Visit the Texas Parks & Wildlife
Department at tpwd.texas.gov

# Cleburne State Park

☐ CAMP CREEK LOOP       1.1 mi.  •  Moderate  •  1 hr.       Date:__________
                                                (round trip)

This short loop follows West Camp Creek, passing bur oaks and Virginia creeper vines along the way. The trail crosses the historic Camp Creek Bridge, built by the Civilian Conservation Corps, with a scenic spot to pause and take in the view.

Trail Notes: _______________________________________________

_______________________________________________

_______________________________________________

☐ FOSSIL RIDGE TRAIL     2.5 mi.  •  Challenging  •  1.5 hrs.     Date:__________
                          (one way)                  (one way)

This trail rises and dips along the park's boundary, offering changing views and a mix of scenic landscapes. Hikers can extend their route by linking up with the Camp Creek Loop or the Coyote Run Nature Trail.

Trail Notes: _______________________________________________

_______________________________________________

_______________________________________________

☐ WHITE-TAIL
  HOLLOW TRAIL          1.9 mi.  •   Easy   •  1.25 hrs.   Date:__________
                        (round trip)               (round trip)

The trail begins with a quiet walk through wooded scenery and finishes with an overlook of Cedar Lake as it crosses a historic dam constructed by the Civilian Conservation Corps.

Trail Notes: _______________________________________________

_______________________________________________

_______________________________________________

☐ SPILLWAY TRAIL        0.7 mi.  •  Moderate  •  1 hr.       Date:__________
                        (one way)              (round trip)

This trail offers the best vantage point of the impressive three-tiered spillway, hand-cut from Comanche Peak limestone by the Civilian Conservation Corps.

Trail Notes: _______________________________________________

_______________________________________________

_______________________________________________

*Continued on next page*  

# Cleburne State Park

☐ **COYOTE RUN NATURE TRAIL** — 1.1 mi. (one way) • Moderate • 1 hr. (round trip)   Date:__________

This nature trail is popular with both hikers and cyclists, offering lake views from limestone hilltops and connections to the Spillway and Fossil Ridge trails.

Trail Notes: ________________________________________________

________________________________________________

________________________________________________

☐ **LIMESTONE RIDGE TRAIL with** — 1.7 mi. (one way) • • 1 hr. (round trip)   Date:__________

☐ **INNER LOOP TRAIL** — 1.7 mi. (one way) • Challenging • 2 hr. (round trip)   Date:__________

This demanding trail winds along rugged limestone cliffs with tight, twisting switchbacks. It's a favorite among cyclists, but hikers should stay alert and use a map or GPS to avoid losing their way. For a longer route, connect to the Inner Loop Trail.

Trail Notes: ________________________________________________

________________________________________________

________________________________________________

☐ **CRAPPIE COVE FISHING TRAIL** — 0.3 mi. (one way) • Easy • 15 min. (one way)   Date:__________

Popular with local anglers, Crappie Cove features rocky shorelines and deep pools that create excellent conditions for a productive day of fishing.

Trail Notes: ________________________________________________

________________________________________________

________________________________________________

☐ **PERCH POINT FISHING TRAIL** — 0.1 mi. (one way) • Easy • 10 min. (one way)   Date:__________

Rocky shorelines along this trail provide ideal habitat for redear sunfish, bass, and catfish.

Trail Notes: ________________________________________________

________________________________________________

________________________________________________

# Cleburne State Park

☐ **SANDY FLATS FISHING TRAIL**    0.2 mi. (one way) • Easy • 15 min. (one way)    Date:________

This shoreline walk between the boat ramp and the beach area leads to shady spots ideal for fishing or simply unwinding.

Trail Notes: ________________________________________

____________________________________________________

____________________________________________________

☐ **BLUECAT BOTTOMS FISHING TRAIL**    0.2 mi. (one way) • Easy • 15 min. (one way)    Date:________

This trail follows the deeper waters of Cedar Lake, where anglers can find fishing spots known for catfish, crappie, and bass.

Trail Notes: ________________________________________

____________________________________________________

____________________________________________________

## 📍 Trailward Finds

☐ **CCC SPILLWAY**
DATE:

☐ **CAMP CREEK DAY-USE AREA**
DATE:

☐ **CAMP CREEK BRIDGE**
DATE:

☐ **PARK ROAD 21 OVERLOOK**
DATE:

☐ **CRAPPIE COVE FISHING AREA**
DATE:

☐ **CEDAR LAKE BEACH**
DATE:

Park Website     Trail Map

Visit the Texas Parks & Wildlife Department at tpwd.texas.gov

# Cooper Lake State Park
## South Sulphur Unit Trails

☐ **COYOTE RUN TRAIL**     4.6 mi. • Moderate • 3 hrs.     Date:_________
(round trip)

This trail explores the rolling hills and low-lying areas of the South Sulphur River watershed. Abundant water, plants, and wildlife once drew both Native peoples and early settlers to this landscape. Along the route, hikers can observe canebrakes and small pocket prairies.

Trail Notes: _________________________________________________

_____________________________________________________________

_____________________________________________________________

☐ **HONEY CREEK INTERPRETIVE TRAIL**     0.3 mi. •     Easy     • 30 min.     Date:_________

This short trail highlights the area's variety of native trees and shrubs and is well suited for families of all ages.

Trail Notes: _________________________________________________

_____________________________________________________________

_____________________________________________________________

☐ **LITTLE BLUESTEM LOOP**     3.1 mi. •     Easy     • 2 hrs.     Date:_________

Designed for beginners, this trail passes through pockets of little bluestem and ends with wide views of the lake. Wildlife tracks are often visible along the route, and the trail connects to three additional paths within the Buggy Whip Trail System.

Trail Notes: _________________________________________________

_____________________________________________________________

_____________________________________________________________

☐ **LONESOME DOVE LOOP**     4.8 mi. •     Moderate/ Challenging     • 3 hrs.     Date:_________

This long loop crosses multiple creeks and passes a peaceful pond along the way. Frequent changes in terrain and elevation add variety, ranging from moderate to more demanding sections. The trail is accessed from the Little Bluestem Loop and is part of the Buggy Whip Trail System.

Trail Notes: _________________________________________________

_____________________________________________________________

_____________________________________________________________

# Cooper Lake State Park
## South Sulphur Unit Trails

☐ **RABBIT RUN**  1.0 mi. • Moderate • 1 hr.  Date:________

These short trails wind beneath post oak groves and through pockets of prairie. They are accessed from the Lonesome Dove Loop and are part of the Buggy Whip Trail System.

Trail Notes: _______________________________________________

_______________________________________________________________

_______________________________________________________________

☐ **PIONEER PASS**  1.5 mi. • Moderate • 1.5 hrs.  Date:________

Sections of this trail feature milkweed and are frequented by monarch butterflies. An old roadbed, once used by local residents before the park was established, is still visible along the route. The trail is accessed from the Lonesome Dove Loop and is part of the Buggy Whip Trail System.

Trail Notes: _______________________________________________

_______________________________________________________________

_______________________________________________________________

☐ **CONNECTOR TRAIL**  0.3 mi.  Date:________

Trail Notes: _______________________________________________

_______________________________________________________________

_______________________________________________________________

## 📍 Trailward Finds

☐ **SUNSET COVE**
DATE:

☐ **CORRAL**
DATE:

☐ **OLD FENCING**
DATE:

☐ **THE CANEBRAKE**
DATE:

☐ **POCKET PRAIRIE**
DATE:

☐ **HARPER'S HILL**
DATE:

Park Website  Trail Map

Visit the Texas Parks & Wildlife
Department at tpwd.texas.gov

# Cooper Lake State Park
## Doctors Creek Unit Trails

☐ **CEDAR CREEK NORTH LOOP**    0.6 mi. •    Easy    • 40 min.    Date:_________

This trail leads into the South Loop, using numbered markers to highlight trees and other plant life along the way. Near a dead oak, look for unusual mushrooms—an example of how even fallen trees continue to support a thriving ecosystem.

Trail Notes: _______________________________________________

_______________________________________________

_______________________________________________

☐ **CEDAR CREEK SOUTH LOOP**    0.5 mi. •    Easy    • 30 min.    Date:_________

This trail leads to the leopard frog marsh, passing through wooded areas where vultures often perch and lively pocket prairies along the way. Just off the main path, hikers can enjoy views of the lakeshore.

Trail Notes: _______________________________________________

_______________________________________________

_______________________________________________

☐ **CEDAR CREEK EAST LOOP**    1.3 mi. •    Easy    • 1 hr. 25 min.    Date:_________

This trail is ideal for wildlife watching, passing through open prairies filled with wildflowers and marshy grasslands. The route leads to a secluded view of the levee, where deer are often seen and hawks circle overhead.

Trail Notes: _______________________________________________

_______________________________________________

_______________________________________________

# Cooper Lake State Park
## Doctors Creek Unit Trails

☐ **CEDAR CREEK WEST LOOP**     0.6 mi.  •     Easy     • 35 min.     Date:_________

This trail passes beneath twisted, mature oak trees, where owls are often heard after dusk. Along the way, the path crosses an old farm road and traces remnants of a historic fence line before entering areas of new-growth prairie and woodland.

Trail Notes: _________________________________________________

_________________________________________________

_________________________________________________

## 📍 Trailward Finds

☐ **WETLAND WONDERS**
DATE:

☐ **PAST AND PRESENT**
DATE:

☐ **FROM GRASSLAND TO PASTURE**
DATE:

☐ **IF TREES COULD TALK**
DATE:

☐ **WATER IS LIFE**
DATE:

☐ **MIGHTY OAKS**
DATE:

Park Website     Trail Map

Visit the Texas Parks & Wildlife
Department at tpwd.texas.gov

# Dinosaur Valley State Park

☐ **LIMESTONE LEDGE TRAIL** (hiking only)   1.6 mi. • Moderate • 2 hrs.   Date:_________

Expect a river crossing along the Paluxy River before reaching the Main Track Site, where paleontologist R.T. Bird uncovered the world's first known sauropod trackway.

Trail Notes: ______________________________________________________

_________________________________________________________________

_________________________________________________________________

☐ **CEDAR BRAKE OUTER LOOP**   7.5 mi. • Challenging • 3.5 hrs.   Date:_________

This extended loop circles the park along limestone ridges topped with dense cedar stands.

Trail Notes: ______________________________________________________

_________________________________________________________________

_________________________________________________________________

☐ **BLACK-CAPPED VIREO TRAIL**   2.7 mi. • Moderate • 1.25 hrs.   Date:_________

These shrubby woodlands provide nesting habitat for black-capped vireos.

Trail Notes: ______________________________________________________

_________________________________________________________________

_________________________________________________________________

☐ **DENIO TRAIL**   1.6 mi. • Moderate • 45 min.   Date:_________

This winding trail follows Denio Creek and offers opportunities to spot the endangered golden-cheeked warbler.

Trail Notes: ______________________________________________________

_________________________________________________________________

_________________________________________________________________

☐ **BUCKEYE TRAIL**   1.4 mi. • Moderate • 45 min.   Date:________

This trail follows Buckeye Creek, where small waterfalls may appear after rainfall.

Trail Notes: ______________________________________________________

_________________________________________________________________

_________________________________________________________________

# Dinosaur Valley State Park

☐ ROCKY RIDGE TRAIL     1.0 mi. • Moderate • 30 min.     Date:___________

This high ridge trail features scenic overlooks with wide-ranging views worth pausing to enjoy.

Trail Notes: ________________________________________________

________________________________________________

________________________________________________

☐ OAK SPRINGS TRAIL     0.3 mi. •     Easy     • 10 min.     Date:___________

This winding trail passes through oak woodlands, where natural springs occasionally bubble up along the route.

Trail Notes: ________________________________________________

________________________________________________

________________________________________________

☐ OVERLOOK TRAIL     0.5 mi. • Challenging • 30 min.     Date:___________
(hiking only)

The overlook rewards the climb with sweeping views of the Paluxy River Valley.

Trail Notes: ________________________________________________

________________________________________________

________________________________________________

☐ HORSESHOE EQUESTRIAN TRAIL     3.1 mi. • Moderate • 1 hr.     Date:___________
(no biking)

This trail follows the edge of the Paluxy River through stretches of bluestem grassland.

Trail Notes: ________________________________________________

________________________________________________

________________________________________________

☐ PALUXY RIVER TRAIL   2.0 mi. •     Easy     • 1.3 hrs.     Date:___________

This trail meanders along a limestone ledge beside the Paluxy River, where a variety of dinosaur tracks can be seen.

Trail Notes: ________________________________________________

________________________________________________

________________________________________________

*Continued on next page*     19

# Dinosaur Valley State Park

☐ **MONARCH TRAIL**   0.5 mi.  •   Easy   • 15 min.   Date:__________

As the trail passes through wooded areas, watch for birds and butterflies moving through the trees.

Trail Notes: ________________________________________________

________________________________________________

________________________________________________

☐ **DISCOVERY LOOP TRAIL**   0.1 mi.  •   Easy   • 10 min.   Date:__________

This easy trail offers a great way to introduce kids to the basics of nature and outdoor exploration.

Trail Notes: ________________________________________________

________________________________________________

________________________________________________

☐ **AMPHITHEATER TRAIL**   0.3 mi.   Date:__________

Trail Notes: ________________________________________________

________________________________________________

________________________________________________

## 📍 Trailward Finds

☐ **DINOSAUR MODELS**
DATE:

☐ **MAIN TRACK SITE**
DATE:

☐ **BLUE HOLE**
DATE:

☐ **BALLROOM TRACK SITE**
DATE:

☐ **PALUXY RIVER SCENIC OVERLOOK**
DATE:

Park Website     Trail Map

Visit the Texas Parks & Wildlife
Department at tpwd.texas.gov

# Eisenhower State Park

☐ **ARMADILLO HILL TRAIL**     0.8 mi. • Moderate • 30 min.     Date:___________

Between markers 1 and 2, this section of the trail passes through woodland, lakeshore, and prairie habitats, highlighting local geology and plant life. Benches along the way offer places to pause and watch for red-bellied woodpeckers, bobcats, or coyotes.

Trail Notes: _______________________________________________

_______________________________________________

_______________________________________________

☐ **IKE'S HIKE AND BIKE TRAIL**     3.2 mi. • Easy to Moderate • 4 hrs.     Date:___________

Between markers 3 and 14, the trail includes a particularly rugged stretch between markers 3 and 4. This challenging section is best suited for experienced hikers and cyclists seeking a more demanding route.

Trail Notes: _______________________________________________

_______________________________________________

_______________________________________________

☐ **PEE WEE PRACTICE AREA**     0.3 mi. • Easy • 1 hr.     Date:___________

This flat, easy section near the entrance of the Ironweed OHV Trail System is well suited for beginner riders. More experienced riders are encouraged to yield to newcomers or choose one of the more advanced routes.

Trail Notes: _______________________________________________

_______________________________________________

_______________________________________________

☐ **BLACKLAND RAMBLE OHV TRAIL**     0.6 mi. • Moderate • 1 hr. to a full day     Date:___________

This portion of the Ironweed OHV Trail System offers open prairie views from a clearing. Rocky areas along the route contain fossils, making it especially important to remain on the trail.

Trail Notes: _______________________________________________

_______________________________________________

_______________________________________________

*Continued on next page*     21

# Eisenhower State Park

☐ **BIG WOODS CANYON OHV TRAIL** — 0.7 mi. • Moderate to Challenging • 1 hr. to a full day — Date:__________

This segment of the Ironweed OHV Trail System passes through both Crosstimbers and Blackland Prairie landscapes. Large oak trees grow in the lower ravines, while higher ground opens into small meadows filled with grasses and wildflowers.

Trail Notes: ________________________________________

________________________________________

________________________________________

☐ **TIMBER RATTLER RUN OHV TRAIL** — 0.7 mi. • Moderate to Challenging • 1 hr. to a full day — Date:__________

This section of the Ironweed OHV Trail System is best traveled at a slower pace, as threatened timber rattlesnakes may be present. The most demanding feature is a steep, narrow stream crossing.

Trail Notes: ________________________________________

________________________________________

________________________________________

☐ **MAIN OHV TRAIL ACCESS** — 0.7 mi. — Date:__________

Trail Notes: ________________________________________

________________________________________

________________________________________

☐ **IRONWEED OHV TRAIL SYSTEM** (motorized only) — 3.3 mi. — Date:__________

Trail Notes: ________________________________________

________________________________________

________________________________________

## 📍 Trailward Finds

☐ **BUTTONBUSH SCENIC POINT**
DATE:

☐ **FIVE-STAR RED OAK**
DATE:

☐ **AMMONITE CROSSING**
DATE:

☐ **LOVER'S LEAP**
DATE:

Park Website　　Trail Map
Visit the Texas Parks & Wildlife
Department at tpwd.texas.gov

# Fort Richardson State Park & Historic Site

☐ **RUMBLING SPRING TRAIL** — 0.5 mi. • Moderate — Date:_________

This winding, scenic trail leads to natural springs, with uneven footing that requires careful steps.

Trail Notes: ___________________________________________________

_____________________________________________________________

_____________________________________________________________

☐ **PRICKLY PEAR TRAIL** — 1.3 mi. • Moderate — Date:_________

This level trail crosses open prairie, offering opportunities to watch for wildlife along the way.

Trail Notes: ___________________________________________________

_____________________________________________________________

_____________________________________________________________

☐ **LOST CREEK NATURE TRAIL** — 0.5 mi. • Easy — Date:_________

This family-friendly nature trail leads to scenic views of Lost Creek.

Trail Notes: ___________________________________________________

_____________________________________________________________

_____________________________________________________________

☐ **KICKING BIRD TRAIL** — 0.3 mi. • Easy — Date:_________

This loop trail offers excellent birdwatching opportunities and is named in honor of the Kiowa chief Kicking Bird.

Trail Notes: ___________________________________________________

_____________________________________________________________

_____________________________________________________________

☐ **LOST CREEK RESERVOIR STATE TRAILWAY** — 9.0 mi. • Moderate — Date:_________

This scenic multi-use trail follows Lost Creek between Fort Richardson State Park & Historic Site and Lost Creek Reservoir, welcoming hikers, cyclists, and equestrians.

Trail Notes: ___________________________________________________

_____________________________________________________________

_____________________________________________________________

*Continued on next page* 

# Fort Richardson State Park & Historic Site

☐ OAK RIDGE TRAIL          0.4 mi.  •  Moderate                Date:____________

This loop trail winds through tree-lined sections between the trailhead parking area and the shoreline of Lost Creek Reservoir.

Trail Notes: ______________________________________________________

_________________________________________________________________

_________________________________________________________________

☐ RESTROOM TRAIL          0.04 mi.                              Date:____________

Trail Notes: ______________________________________________________

_________________________________________________________________

_________________________________________________________________

## 📍 Trailward Finds

☐ **FORT RICHARDSON COMMISSARY**
DATE:

☐ **RUMBLING SPRING**
DATE:

☐ **FLOUR MILL VIEW**
DATE:

☐ **CHICAGO, ROCK ISLAND & TEXAS RAILROAD DEPO**
DATE:

Park Website          Trail Map

Visit the Texas Parks & Wildlife
Department at tpwd.texas.gov

# Lake Mineral Wells State Park

☐ **RED WATERFRONT TRAIL** (hiking only)   0.8 mi. • Moderate • 45 min.   Date:_________

This trail traces the eastern shoreline of Lake Mineral Wells to Penitentiary Hollow, where steep rock walls form a distinctive wildlife habitat and a popular destination for rock climbers.

Trail Notes: _______________________________________________

_______________________________________________

_______________________________________________

☐ **BLUE WATERFRONT TRAIL** (hiking only)   1.5 mi. • Moderate • 1 hr.   Date:_________

This winding trail follows the lake's western shoreline, passing screened shelters and camping loops along the way. Binoculars are helpful for viewing wildlife near the Plateau Camping Loop.

Trail Notes: _______________________________________________

_______________________________________________

_______________________________________________

☐ **PRIMITIVE CAMPING TRAIL** (hiking only)   2.0 mi. • Moderate • 1.5 hrs.   Date:_________

This steep, rocky trail requires careful footing as it passes through a remnant of the ancient Western Cross Timbers forest. Beyond the trees, the landscape opens into grasslands similar to those that once drew early cattlemen to the area.

Trail Notes: _______________________________________________

_______________________________________________

_______________________________________________

☐ **CROSS TIMBERS BLACK TRAIL** (multiuse)   2.3 mi. • Easy • 2 hrs.   Date:_________

This trail explores the Lost Lake wetlands, an area that once formed part of Fort Wolters, a U.S. Army training center during the 20th century. Remnants of former fort buildings are still visible along the route.

Trail Notes: _______________________________________________

_______________________________________________

_______________________________________________

☐ **CROSS TIMBERS GREEN TRAIL** (multiuse)   1.5 mi. • Easy • 1 hr.   Date:_________

As the Green Cross Timbers Trail winds through a grassland savanna, the plant life along the route gradually shifts and changes.

Trail Notes: _______________________________________________

_______________________________________________

_______________________________________________

*Continued on next page*   

# Lake Mineral Wells State Park

☐ **CROSS TIMBERS ORANGE TRAIL** (multiuse)  1.3 mi.  •  Easy  •  1 hr.  Date:__________

This trail follows Rock Creek as it winds through the landscape, with opportunities to spot wildlife tracks or other signs of animal activity near the creek crossing.

Trail Notes: ______________________________________________
______________________________________________
______________________________________________

☐ **CROSS TIMBERS YELLOW TRAIL** (multiuse)  1.6 mi.  •  Easy  •  1.25 hrs.  Date:__________

Along the route, hikers will pass an old paved military road once used by soldiers training at Fort Wolters.

Trail Notes: ______________________________________________
______________________________________________
______________________________________________

☐ **CROSS TIMBERS MAROON TRAIL** (multiuse)  2.2 mi.  •  Moderate  •  1.75 hrs.  Date:__________

Heading east, the trail follows a high ridge with views over the valley before descending into a natural low area as it turns south.

Trail Notes: ______________________________________________
______________________________________________
______________________________________________

☐ **TRAILWAY SPUR** (multiuse)  0.6 mi.  •  Moderate  •  30 min.  Date:__________

This route connects to the Lake Mineral Wells State Park Trailway, following a historic rail corridor for nearly 20 miles between Weatherford and Mineral Wells.

Trail Notes: ______________________________________________
______________________________________________
______________________________________________

## 📍 Trailward Finds

☐ **THE FOUR CEDAR ELMS**
DATE:

☐ **POST OAKS**
DATE:

☐ **PENITENTIARY HOLLOW OVERLOOK**
DATE:

☐ **ROCK CREEK**
DATE:

Park Website     Trail Map
Visit the Texas Parks & Wildlife Department at tpwd.texas.gov

# Palo Pinto Mountains State Park

☐ RAPTOR RIDGE TRAIL 0.5 mi. • Easy • 30 min. Date:__________
(1 mi. round-trip)

This accessible trail gently winds past scenic overlooks, with quiet resting spots beneath juniper trees where native songbirds can often be heard. Horses are not permitted.

Trail Notes: __________________________________________________

__________________________________________________

__________________________________________________

☐ CONNECTING TRAIL 0.5 mi. • Easy • 20 min. Date:__________

This accessible trail connects Canyon View Day-Use Area with Painted Stick Campground or the Main Trailhead. Horses are not permitted.

Trail Notes: __________________________________________________

__________________________________________________

__________________________________________________

☐ TUCKER LAKE TRAIL 4.5 mi. • Moderate • 2 hrs. 30 min. Date:__________

This demanding route climbs and descends around the hills and limestone cliffs near Tucker Lake and Russell Creek, so carrying plenty of water is essential.

Trail Notes: __________________________________________________

__________________________________________________

__________________________________________________

☐ CROSS TIMBERS TRAIL 2.0 mi. • Easy • 1 hr. Date:__________
(one way)

This uphill stretch climbs from Russell Creek to the Main Trailhead, making hydration especially important. Along the edge of Canyon View, watch for deer and woodpeckers moving through the area.

Trail Notes: __________________________________________________

__________________________________________________

__________________________________________________

*Continued on next page*  

# Palo Pinto Mountains State Park

☐ **BEN'S TRAIL**   0.8 mi. • Moderate • 30 min.   Date:__________

This loop circles Lake Tucker, following the cliffs above Russell Creek and offering scenic lake views. Seasonal birdsong often carries across the hills along the way.

Trail Notes: ________________________________________________

________________________________________________________________

________________________________________________________________

☐ **LAKESHORE ACCESSIBLE**   0.2 mi. •   Easy   • 15 min.   Date:__________

This short, accessible trail passes through the historic remains of former vacation cottages. In spring, distinctive plants add bursts of color and fragrant blooms along the route. Horses are not permitted.

Trail Notes: ________________________________________________

________________________________________________________________

________________________________________________________________

☐ **BUTTONBUSH TRAIL**   0.7 mi. •   Easy   • 45 min.   Date:__________
(1.3 mi. round-trip)

Beginning at the Tucker Lake Dam, the trail descends along the shoreline to a shady mesquite grove. Tall reeds and cattails along the water's edge provide cover for a variety of waterfowl.

Trail Notes: ________________________________________________

________________________________________________________________

________________________________________________________________

☐ **PALO PINTO CREEK LOOP**   1.3 mi. •   Easy   • 45 min.   Date:__________
(from trailhead)

Expect multiple creek crossings on this well-shaded trail as it weaves back and forth across Palo Pinto Creek. In summer, water levels are often low, but recent rainfall can bring the creek to life.

Trail Notes: ________________________________________________

________________________________________________________________

________________________________________________________________

# Palo Pinto Mountains State Park

☐ **TEXAS & PACIFIC TRAIL**  5.7 mi. • Moderate • 5 hrs. 30 min.  Date:__________
(11 mi. round-trip)

Be sure to carry plenty of water as the trail descends from the Palo Pinto Creek canyon into open prairies and shaded corridors of trees. The western stretches offer a rugged landscape that captures the spirit of the Old West.

Trail Notes: ___________________________________________________

___________________________________________________

___________________________________________________

## 📍 Trailward Finds

☐ **SUNSET WATCH**
DATE:

☐ **MESQUITE GROVE**
DATE:

☐ **LIMESTONE SINKHOLE**
DATE:

☐ **RUSSELL CREEK OVERLOOK**
DATE:

☐ **CANYON VIEW OVERLOOK**
DATE:

☐ **WILDFLOWER PRAIRIE**
DATE:

☐ **ROCKY BOTTOM**
DATE:

☐ **RAGSDALE CABIN**
DATE:

Park Website    Trail Map
Visit the Texas Parks & Wildlife
Department at tpwd.texas.gov

# Possum Kingdom State Park

☐ LAKEVIEW TRAIL          1.4 mi.  •  Moderate          Date:_________

This winding trail passes through a mix of woodlands and prairies, with spring bringing a colorful display of wildflowers along the route.

Trail Notes: ______________________________________________

_____________________________________________________________

_____________________________________________________________

☐ LONGHORN TRAIL          0.4 mi.  •  Challenging          Date:_________

This rugged trail climbs to an overlook with sweeping views of the park and Possum Kingdom Lake.

Trail Notes: ______________________________________________

_____________________________________________________________

_____________________________________________________________

☐ CHAPARRAL RIDGE TRAIL          0.5 mi.  •  Challenging          Date:_________

This steep trail requires careful footing as it climbs through juniper woodlands and passes several scenic overlooks.

Trail Notes: ______________________________________________

_____________________________________________________________

_____________________________________________________________

☐ CCC CAMP TRAIL          0.6 mi.  •  Easy          Date:_________

This trail traces the remaining features of a former Civilian Conservation Corps camp once located in Possum Kingdom State Park, offering a glimpse into the park's early history.

Trail Notes: ______________________________________________

_____________________________________________________________

_____________________________________________________________

## 📍 Trailward Finds

☐ LONGHORN TRAIL OVERLOOK
DATE:

☐ PARK CONCESSION
DATE:

☐ FISH SCULPTURE
DATE:

☐ CAMPGROUND TRAIL OVERLOOK
DATE:

☐ CCC CAMP SITE
DATE:

Park Website          Trail Map

Visit the Texas Parks & Wildlife Department at tpwd.texas.gov

# Purtis Creek State Park

☐ SOLAR WALK TRAIL · 0.5 mi. · Easy · 30 min. · Date:_________

This short, paved trail follows the dam and features interpretive signs that illustrate the relative distances of the planets from the sun.

Trail Notes: _______________________________________________

_______________________________________________

_______________________________________________

☐ BEAVER SLIDE NATURE PATH · 1.3 mi. · Easy · 1.5 hrs. · Date:_________

This popular trail features sweeping lake views and frequent opportunities to observe wildlife along the way. Bicycles are not permitted on this trail.

Trail Notes: _______________________________________________

_______________________________________________

_______________________________________________

☐ WOLFPEN HIKE AND BIKE TRAIL (GREEN LOOP) · 0.8 mi. (one way) · Easy · 45 min. · Date:_________

This short, family-friendly trail is ideal for young children and works well for both hiking and biking. It provides access to the remaining loops of the Wolfpen Trail.

Trail Notes: _______________________________________________

_______________________________________________

_______________________________________________

☐ WOLFPEN HIKE AND BIKE TRAIL (BLUE LOOP) · 2.0 mi. · Easy · 2 hrs. · Date:_________

This shaded section of the Wolfpen Trail is well suited for hiking or biking, especially on warm, sunny days.

Trail Notes: _______________________________________________

_______________________________________________

_______________________________________________

*Continued on next page* 

# Purtis Creek State Park

☐ **WOLFPEN HIKE AND BIKE TRAIL** (RED LOOP)　　1.2 mi.　•　Easy　•　1.5 hrs.　Date:___________

This third segment of the Wolfpen Trail includes gentle elevation changes and is suitable for both hiking and biking. Wildlife sightings are possible along the way.

Trail Notes: _______________________________________________

_______________________________________________

_______________________________________________

## 📍 Trailward Finds

☐ **BLUESTEM PRAIRIE**
DATE:

☐ **ENTRANCE TO OAK FOREST**
DATE:

☐ **BENT BY NATURE**
DATE:

☐ **NATIVE WATER PLANTS RESTORATION**
DATE:

☐ **FEATHERED FRIENDS**
DATE:

☐ **BURLWOOD TREE**
DATE:

☐ **A PLACE TO REST**
DATE:

Park Website　　　Trail Map
Visit the Texas Parks & Wildlife
Department at tpwd.texas.gov

# Ray Roberts Lake State Park
### Isle du Bois and Jordan Unit

☐ **EAGLE ACTIVITY TRAIL**     0.3 mi.  •  Easy          Date:__________

This self-guided trail invites kids and families to move like animals—jump like a frog, scurry like a squirrel, and try other hands-on challenges along the way.

Trail Notes: _________________________________________________

_____________________________________________________________

_____________________________________________________________


☐ **LOST PINES TRAIL**     0.5 mi.  •  Easy          Date:__________

This half-mile loop offers brief lake views, passes the remains of an early settler's cabin, and winds through tall pines mixed with native oaks and elms.

Trail Notes: _________________________________________________

_____________________________________________________________

_____________________________________________________________


☐ **RANDY BELL SCENIC TRAIL**     2.2 mi.  •  Easy          Date:__________

This paved trail shares stories of the landscape while guiding visitors through woodlands and prairies much as they appeared before the development of Ray Roberts Lake.

Trail Notes: _________________________________________________

_____________________________________________________________

_____________________________________________________________


☐ **WAGON WHEEL CROSSING**     3.6 mi.  •  Moderate          Date:__________
(one way)

This trail system links the Bluestem parking area with the Horse Blaze Trail along the FM 455 section of the Greenbelt, providing access to additional Greenbelt routes. Potable water is not available along this trail.

Trail Notes: _________________________________________________

_____________________________________________________________

_____________________________________________________________

*Continued on next page*     

# Ray Roberts Lake State Park
## Isle du Bois and Jordan Unit

☐ REDBUD RUN    4.5 mi. • Easy    Date:___________

This mostly level, multi-use equestrian trail follows the shoreline. Potable water is not available along the route.

Trail Notes: __________________________________________

__________________________________________

__________________________________________


☐ ROCKY SPUR    3.0 mi. • Moderate    Date:___________

This challenging trail features sandstone formations, rugged terrain, and frequent elevation changes. Potable water is not available along the route.

Trail Notes: __________________________________________

__________________________________________

__________________________________________


☐ DORBA TRAIL LOOP A    0.2 mi. • Moderate    Date:___________

Named for the Dallas Off-Road Bicycle Association, this trail is part of a series built by mountain bikers. It is the shortest of the DORBA loops, making it a good choice for beginners or a quick warm-up ride.

Trail Notes: __________________________________________

__________________________________________

__________________________________________


☐ DORBA TRAIL LOOP B    0.7 mi. • Moderate    Date:___________

At under a mile in length, this segment makes a natural next step after completing Loop A.

Trail Notes: __________________________________________

__________________________________________

__________________________________________

# Ray Roberts Lake State Park
## Isle du Bois and Jordan Unit

☐ DORBA TRAIL LOOP C  3.7 mi.  •  Moderate  Date:__________
(4.4 mi. RT)

This trail makes up the middle stretch of the DORBA loop system.

Trail Notes: _______________________________________________

_______________________________________________

_______________________________________________

☐ DORBA TRAIL LOOP D  2.6 mi.  •  Moderate  Date:__________
(7.0 mi. RT)

Note: D Loop — experts only.

Trail Notes: _______________________________________________

_______________________________________________

_______________________________________________

☐ DORBA TRAIL LOOP E  2.3 mi.  •  Moderate  Date:__________
(9.3 mi. RT)

This final loop completes nearly 10 miles within the trail system.

Trail Notes: _______________________________________________

_______________________________________________

_______________________________________________

## 📍 Trailward Finds

☐ **WINDOW INTO THE PAST**
DATE:

☐ **LAKESIDE LIFE**
DATE:

☐ **NATURE CENTER**
DATE:

☐ **POCKET PRAIRIES**
DATE:

Park Website     Trail Map
Visit the Texas Parks & Wildlife
Department at tpwd.texas.gov

# Ray Roberts Lake State Park
## Johnson Branch Unit

☐ **DOGWOOD CANYON TRAIL**   2.6 mi. (one way)  •  Moderate   Date:_________

This primitive trail winds through Cross Timbers woodlands and pockets of native prairie, offering a changing mix of scenery. Water is not available along the route.

Trail Notes: ___________________________________________

_______________________________________________________

_______________________________________________________

☐ **KID FISH POND TRAIL**   0.5 mi.  •   Easy   Date:_________

This easy loop circles the Kid Fish Pond and is perfect for a leisurely walk. After your stroll, grab a fishing pole and try your luck along the water's edge.

Trail Notes: ___________________________________________

_______________________________________________________

_______________________________________________________

☐ **CROSS TIMBERS TRAIL**   2.8 mi.  •   Easy   Date:_________

This paved trail is well suited for visitors of all ages and can be accessed from most camping loops, making it easy to begin exploring right away.

Trail Notes: ___________________________________________

_______________________________________________________

_______________________________________________________

☐ **DORBA TRAIL BLUE LOOP**   1.1 mi.  •  Moderate   Date:_________

Named for the Dallas Off-Road Bicycle Association, this loop is part of a six-trail system built by mountain bikers. As the shortest of the DORBA loops, it's a great option for beginners or a warm-up ride.

Trail Notes: ___________________________________________

_______________________________________________________

_______________________________________________________

# Ray Roberts Lake State Park
## Johnson Branch Unit

☐ **DORBA TRAIL ORANGE/PINK LOOPS**   2.0 mi. (3.1 mi. RT) • Moderate     Date:__________

These are the second and third loops of the DORBA Trail. The orange loop spans about 1.3 miles, while the pink loop adds just over 0.3 miles, making it an easy extension. Scenic views can be found along both routes.

Trail Notes: ________________________________________________

_______________________________________________________________

_______________________________________________________________

☐ **DORBA TRAIL GREEN LOOP**   1.8 mi. (4.9 mi. RT) • Moderate     Date:__________

This is one of the easier loops in the system and can be reached from the pink or orange loops, or by connecting via the Dogwood Canyon Trail.

Trail Notes: ________________________________________________

_______________________________________________________________

_______________________________________________________________

☐ **DORBA TRAIL RED/YELLOW LOOPS**   4.0 mi. (8.8 mi. RT) • Challenging     Date:__________

These final two segments of the DORBA Trail deliver demanding riding as they weave through prairies and timbered areas.
Note: The Red segment is intended for expert riders only.

Trail Notes: ________________________________________________

_______________________________________________________________

_______________________________________________________________

# ◉ Trailward Finds

☐ **REFLECTION BENCH**
DATE:

☐ **DORBA TRAILHEAD**
DATE:

☐ **CORRAL**
DATE:

☐ **KID FISH POND**
DATE:

☐ **WOLF ISLAND VIEW**
DATE:

**Park Website**     **Trail Map**
Visit the Texas Parks & Wildlife
Department at tpwd.texas.gov

# EAST TEXAS
## REGION

| TRAILS TO EXPLORE | PARKS INCLUDED |
|:---:|:---:|
| 91 | 12 |

## Regional Milestones

☐ First Park Completed

Trail: _________________

Date: _________________

☐ Final Park Completed

Trail: _________________

Date: _________________

☐ Favorite Trail

Trail: _________________

Date: _________________

☐ Longest Trail Completed

Sandy Creek Paddling Trail

Date: _________________

☐ Shortest Trail Completed

Fire Tower Trail

Date: _________________

☐ Most Challenging Trail Completed

Trail: _________________

Date: _________________

## All 91 East Texas Trails Completed

**83.85** Miles Hiked

Date: _________________         Total Miles Hiked: _________________

# Atlanta State Park

☐ **BOBO'S FERRY TRAIL**   0.5 mi. •   Easy   • 20 min.   Date:__________

This short trail starts near park headquarters and follows a historic wagon route before ending at the swim beach parking area.

Trail Notes: _____________________________________________
_____________________________________________
_____________________________________________

☐ **VOLKSMARCH TRAIL**   0.7 mi. •   Easy   • 40 min.   Date:__________

This is the least demanding trail in the park and connects with the Arrowhead Trail, which leads to a scenic lake overlook.

Trail Notes: _____________________________________________
_____________________________________________
_____________________________________________

☐ **ARROWHEAD TRAIL**   0.8 mi. •   Easy   • 30 min.   Date:__________

This relaxed forest walk leads to a peaceful lakeside view at the shoreline.

Trail Notes: _____________________________________________
_____________________________________________
_____________________________________________

☐ **TERRACE TRAIL**   0.3 mi. •   Easy   • 20 min.   Date:__________

This short trail travels through land that was once used for farming. For a longer outing, carefully cross the park road to connect with the Hickory Hollow Nature Trail.

Trail Notes: _____________________________________________
_____________________________________________
_____________________________________________

☐ **HICKORY HOLLOW NATURE TRAIL**   0.7 mi. • Moderate • 1 hr.   Date:__________

To start and finish at the parking lot, be sure to take the correct turn before entering the White Oak Ridge Trail.

Trail Notes: _____________________________________________
_____________________________________________
_____________________________________________

# Atlanta State Park

☐ **WHITE OAK RIDGE TRAIL**     1.2 mi. • Easy • 45 min.    Date:__________

Beginning near the White Oak restroom at the north end of the trail, this route climbs above the lakeshore and connects to the Hickory Hollow Nature Trail for a longer hike.

Trail Notes: _______________________________________________

_______________________________________________

_______________________________________________

## 📍 Trailward Finds

☐ **WHO TRAVELED HERE?**
DATE:

☐ **FLOOD TO FOREST**
DATE:

☐ **A PEACEFUL PLACE**
DATE:

☐ **SUNSETS, SOARING, AND SQUADRONS**
DATE:

☐ **FROM THE KNIFE-EDGE OF EXTINCTION**
DATE:

Park Website     Trail Map

Visit the Texas Parks & Wildlife Department at tpwd.texas.gov

# Caddo Lake State Park

☐ CADDO FOREST TRAIL  0.7 mi. • Moderate • 1 hr.  Date:__________

This short woodland walk offers a glimpse into both the natural landscape and history of Caddo Lake State Park. Visitors should note that the route includes two stair sections.

Trail Notes: ______________________________________________

__________________________________________________________

__________________________________________________________

☐ PINE RIDGE SPUR  0.2 mi. • Easy • 15 min.  Date:__________

This short connector trail passes through upland pine forest before transitioning into bottomland hardwoods as it joins the Caddo Forest Trail.

Trail Notes: ______________________________________________

__________________________________________________________

__________________________________________________________

☐ PINE RIDGE LOOP  0.8 mi. • Moderate • 1 hr.  Date:__________

For a hillier hike, this trail explores a quieter side of Caddo Lake State Park. Some sections are steep and require careful footing.

Trail Notes: ______________________________________________

__________________________________________________________

__________________________________________________________

☐ CCC CUT-THROUGH  0.2 mi. • Moderate • 15 min.  Date:__________

Though brief, this steep trail includes two staircases, one constructed by the Civilian Conservation Corps. Beginning near the fishing pier, it provides access to the rest of the trail network.

Trail Notes: ______________________________________________

__________________________________________________________

__________________________________________________________

## 📍 Trailward Finds

☐ VIEW OF THE PAST
DATE:

☐ CCCPAVILION
DATE:

☐ SAW MILL POND
DATE:

**Park Website**  **Trail Map**
Visit the Texas Parks & Wildlife
Department at tpwd.texas.gov

# Daingerfield State Park

☐ **RUSTLING LEAVES TRAIL**  2.4 mi. • Moderate • 1.5 hrs.  Date:_________

This peaceful trail winds through towering trees around Little Pine Lake. For a different perspective, be sure to include the peninsula loop on the lake's south side.

Trail Notes: _______________________________________________

_______________________________________________

_______________________________________________

☐ **MOUNTAIN VIEW TRAIL**  0.8 mi. • Challenging • 1 hr.  Date:_________

This demanding trail climbs to one of the area's highest points, rewarding hikers with views of pine-covered bluffs. Some sections are steep and require careful footing.

Trail Notes: _______________________________________________

_______________________________________________

_______________________________________________

## 📍 Trailward Finds

☐ **HISTORIC ENTRY SIGN**
DATE:

☐ **REPURPOSED BOAT HOUSE**
DATE:

☐ **SCENIC VIEW**
DATE:

☐ **BRIDGE AND CCC DAM**
DATE:

☐ **CCC PICNIC AREA**
DATE:

Park Website　　Trail Map

Visit the Texas Parks & Wildlife Department at tpwd.texas.gov

# Fort Boggy State Park

No official **trail map** is available for this park. Use the space below to record your hike time and difficulty

☐ LEON PRAIRIE TRAIL .41 mi. Date:__________

Trail Notes: _______________________________________

___________________________________________________

___________________________________________________

☐ TUNNEL TRAIL .37 mi. Date:__________

Trail Notes: _______________________________________

___________________________________________________

___________________________________________________

☐ CAMPBELL TRAIL 1.17 mi. Date:__________

Trail Notes: _______________________________________

___________________________________________________

___________________________________________________

☐ LAKE TRAIL 1.0 mi. Date:__________

Trail Notes: _______________________________________

___________________________________________________

___________________________________________________

 # Trailward Finds

☐ FISHING PIER
DATE:

☐ SWIMMING AREA
DATE:

Park Website    Park Map

Visit the Texas Parks & Wildlife
Department at tpwd.texas.gov

# Lake Bob Sandlin State Park

☐ LAKEVIEW LOOP        0.6 mi. • Easy • 30 min.    Date:__________

As you walk along the State Park Cove, watch for waterfowl and keep an eye out for a possible bald eagle sighting.

Trail Notes: _______________________________________________

_______________________________________________________________

_______________________________________________________________


☐ BRIM POND TRAIL        0.3 mi. • Moderate • 20 min.    Date:__________

This trail passes through a creekside area where pine trees, American beautyberry, ferns, and buckeye grow, attracting birds and other wildlife to the water. A steep gully crossing adds a more challenging section along the route.

Trail Notes: _______________________________________________

_______________________________________________________________

_______________________________________________________________


☐ HOMESTEAD TRAIL        0.4 mi. • Easy • 20 min.    Date:__________

This route follows land where a family once made their home.

Trail Notes: _______________________________________________

_______________________________________________________________

_______________________________________________________________


☐ DOGWOOD TRAIL        1.7 mi. • Easy • 1 hr.    Date:__________

This forested hike leads to the Trout Pond and is a great option for anglers bringing a fishing pole along the way.

Trail Notes: _______________________________________________

_______________________________________________________________

_______________________________________________________________

*Continued on next page*    

# Lake Bob Sandlin State Park

☐ DOGWOOD CUTOFF    0.3 mi. •    Easy    • 20 min.    Date:___________

This quick forest shortcut is ideal when time is limited. Turning north at either "T" junction leads to the Trout Pond.

Trail Notes: ___________________________________________________

_______________________________________________________________

_______________________________________________________________

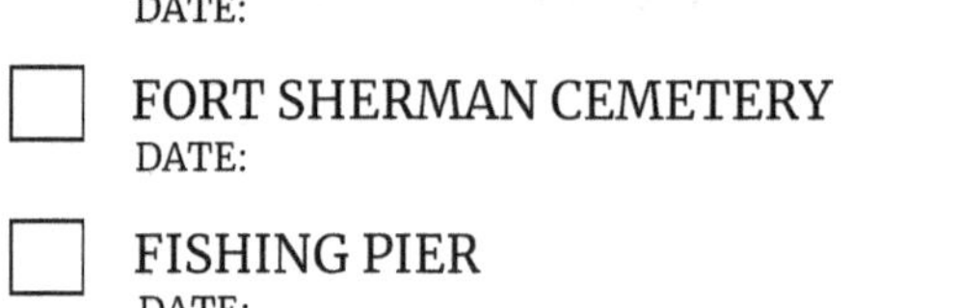 Trailward Finds

☐ **BRIM POND**
DATE:

☐ **FORT SHERMAN CEMETERY**
DATE:

☐ **FISHING PIER**
DATE:

☐ **TROUT POND**
DATE:

Park Website    Trail Map
Visit the Texas Parks & Wildlife
Department at tpwd.texas.gov

# Lake Livingston State Park

☐ **BAKBA TRAIL**      2 mi. • Moderate • 1 hr.     Date:__________

This quiet forest path offers an easy stroll, with opportunities to listen for the rhythmic tapping of woodpeckers.

Trail Notes: ______________________________________________

__________________________________________________________

__________________________________________________________


☐ **PINEYWOODS BOARDWALK TRAIL**     0.9 mi. • Moderate • 30 min.    Date:__________

Just under a mile long, this improved trail provides views of both wetland and woodland habitats.

Trail Notes: ______________________________________________

__________________________________________________________

__________________________________________________________


☐ **TRINITY TRACE TRAIL**      2.1 mi. • Moderate • 2 hrs.    Date:__________

The Trinity Trace Trail links the park's campsites and passes through some of its most scenic forest areas, with frequent opportunities to observe wildlife.

Trail Notes: ______________________________________________

__________________________________________________________

__________________________________________________________


☐ **OAK FLAT TRAIL**      0.3 mi. • Easy • 15 min.    Date:__________

This short, easy path is one of the park's most accessible hikes and offers a clear look at forest succession as it naturally unfolds.

Trail Notes: ______________________________________________

__________________________________________________________

__________________________________________________________

*Continued on next page*    

# Lake Livingston State Park

☐ HAWTHORN TRAIL        0.2 mi. •        Easy        • 20 min.    Date:___________

This short woodland route provides a quick connection from the Trinity Trace Trail to park headquarters.

Trail Notes: _______________________________________________

_______________________________________________

_______________________________________________

☐ FÓ:SI TRAIL        0.5 mi. •  Moderate • 45 min.    Date:___________

Named after a Coushatta word meaning "bird," this half-mile woodland path connects the Oak Flat Trail with the Pineywoods Boardwalk Trail.

Trail Notes: _______________________________________________

_______________________________________________

_______________________________________________

## 📍 Trailward Finds

☐ **WILDLIFE VIEWING AREA**
DATE:

☐ **FROG POND**
DATE:

☐ **OBSERVATION TOWER**
DATE:

☐ **NUTMEG HICKORY**
DATE:

Park Website        Trail Map

Visit the Texas Parks & Wildlife
Department at tpwd.texas.gov

# Lake Tawakoni State Park

☐ **FARKLEBERRY TRAIL**   0.5 mi. •   Easy   • 15 min.   Date:_________

This short connector links three trails. Turn right at the junction to join the Osage Orange Trail, or turn left to extend your hike along the Blackjack Trail.

Trail Notes: _______________________________________________

_______________________________________________

_______________________________________________

☐ **OSAGE ORANGE TRAIL**   0.8 mi. •   Easy   • 20 min.   Date:_________

Named for the fruit of the Osage orange, or bois d'arc tree, this trail connects with the Red Oak Trail before looping back to the crossing. The Osage orange produces a hard, green-yellow fruit about the size of a softball, which serves as an important food source for wildlife in late summer and early fall.

Trail Notes: _______________________________________________

_______________________________________________

_______________________________________________

☐ **RED OAK TRAIL**   0.4 mi. •   Easy   • 15 min.   Date:_________

This tree-lined trail traces the shoreline of Lake Tawakoni, passing through a variety of habitats where wildlife is often active.

Trail Notes: _______________________________________________

_______________________________________________

_______________________________________________

☐ **BLACKJACK TRAIL**   1.5 mi. • Moderate • 2 hrs.   Date:_________

This trail is named for the blackjack oak trees which have grown here for over 50 years. This long, trail will bring you back to the crossing.

Trail Notes: _______________________________________________

_______________________________________________

_______________________________________________

☐ **SPRING POINT BRANCH TRAIL**   0.1 mi. •   Easy   • 5 min.   Date:_________

Spring Point Branch is a short, easy walk through an East Texas hardwood forest. Hikers can turn around at the T-junction or continue on to the Spring Point Trail.

Trail Notes: _______________________________________________

_______________________________________________

_______________________________________________

*Continued on next page*   

# Lake Tawakoni State Park

☐ SPRING POINT TRAIL   0.4 mi. • Moderate • 45 min.   Date:__________

This trail offers excellent birdwatching opportunities, from shaded woodland and pocket prairie to open stretches along the beach.

Trail Notes: _______________________________

_______________________________

_______________________________

☐ SPRING POINT EAST TRAIL   0.4 mi. •   Easy   • 20 min.   Date:__________

This short loop leads out to the point and offers brief views of the lake.

Trail Notes: _______________________________

_______________________________

_______________________________

☐ WHITE DEER TRAIL   0.4 mi. •   Easy   • 45 min.   Date:__________

Tucked away from the campground, this nature trail offers chances for unexpected wildlife sightings.

Trail Notes: _______________________________

_______________________________

_______________________________

## ⚲ Trailward Finds

☐ **GOING GREEN!**
DATE:

☐ **RESTORING A PRAIRIE**
DATE:

☐ **A VIEW OF THE LAKE**
DATE:

☐ **A TEMPORARY GATHERING**
DATE:

☐ **FEATHERED FRIENDS**
DATE:

☐ **BUSTLING BOATS**
DATE:

☐ **PEAR TREES POND**
DATE:

Park Website     Trail Map

Visit the Texas Parks & Wildlife Department at tpwd.texas.gov

# Martin Creek Lake State Park

☐ OLD HENDERSON ROAD LOOP    1.2 mi. • Moderate      Date:__________

This trail follows Old Henderson Road, once a trade route linking the towns of Henderson and Shreveport, offering a glimpse into the area's early history.

Trail Notes: _______________________________________________

_______________________________________________

_______________________________________________

☐ HARMONY HILL LOOP    1.5 mi. •    Easy      Date:__________

This winding forest path traces the edge of the former community of Harmony Hill, now a nationally recognized historic district. Through the trees, hikers may catch glimpses of the town cemetery just beyond the park boundary.

Trail Notes: _______________________________________________

_______________________________________________

_______________________________________________

☐ ISLAND TRAILS    0.9 mi. •    Easy      Date:__________

This trail invites a little adventure as it passes through tall pines and open grasslands, where deer are sometimes spotted. It's fun to wonder how they made their way onto the island.

Trail Notes: _______________________________________________

_______________________________________________

_______________________________________________

## 📍 Trailward Finds

☐ POWER PLANT
DATE:

☐ BIRDING
DATE:

☐ HISTORIC OLD HENDERSON ROAD
DATE:

☐ GAS WELL PUMP
DATE:

☐ PINE PLANTATION
DATE:

☐ HARMONY HILL CEMETERY
DATE:

Park Website      Trail Map
Visit the Texas Parks & Wildlife
Department at tpwd.texas.gov

# Martin Dies, Jr. State Park

☐ WILDLIFE TRAIL          1.4 mi. • Moderate • 1 hr.     Date:_________

The Wildlife Trail passes through a mix of open clearings and dense woodland, crossing both park land and the adjacent wildlife management area.

Trail Notes: _________________________________________________

_________________________________________________________________

_________________________________________________________________

☐ WHITETAIL TRAIL     0.7 mi. •     Easy     • 30 min.   Date:_________

This trail follows a cypress slough and winds through hardwood forest, offering a diverse mix of ecosystems and natural scenery.

Trail Notes: _________________________________________________

_________________________________________________________________

_________________________________________________________________

☐ FOREST TRAIL          1.0 mi. •     Easy     • 45 min.   Date:_________

This trail showcases a wide variety of trees, shrubs, and woody vines that make the walk especially appealing. A plant guide highlighting common species is available on the park's website.

Trail Notes: _________________________________________________

_________________________________________________________________

_________________________________________________________________

☐ ISLAND TRAIL          0.8 mi. • Moderate • 30 min.    Date:_________

Towering beech and pine trees line this trail, while its rolling curves and hills offer a challenge for even experienced cyclists.

Trail Notes: _________________________________________________

_________________________________________________________________

_________________________________________________________________

☐ SANDY CREEK TRAIL  0.8 mi. •     Easy     • 40 min.   Date:_________

This trail follows the eastern shoreline of B.A. Steinhagen Reservoir, exploring the landscape between the state park and Sandy Creek Park, managed by the U.S. Army Corps of Engineers.

Trail Notes: _________________________________________________

_________________________________________________________________

_________________________________________________________________

# Martin Dies, Jr. State Park

☐ SLOUGH TRAIL  2.2 mi. • Moderate • 90 min.  Date:_________

This winding trail passes where several habitats come together, traveling alongside swampy marsh areas and through bottomland hardwoods and dense pine forest. The meeting of these landscapes offers a distinctive look at East Texas biodiversity.

Trail Notes: ________________________________________________

________________________________________________

________________________________________________

☐ SANDY CREEK PADDLING TRAIL  5.4 mi. • Challenging • 2.5 hrs.  Date:_________

As the park's longest paddling route, this trail follows the shoreline before crossing stretches of open water. Two boat ramps along the way provide convenient spots to pull over and take a break.

Trail Notes: ________________________________________________

________________________________________________

________________________________________________

☐ NECHES PADDLING TRAIL  2.8 mi. • Moderate • 90 min.  Date:_________

This buoy-marked route curves toward the Neches River, where paddlers can follow the river's southern current or choose a shorter path into calmer water.

Trail Notes: ________________________________________________

________________________________________________

________________________________________________

☐ WALNUT PADDLING TRAIL  2.7 mi. • Moderate • 90 min.  Date:_________

This paddling route circles the park's Walnut Ridge Unit along the Walnut Paddling Trail, continuing until you pass beneath both the park's observation bridge and the road bridge.

Trail Notes: ________________________________________________

________________________________________________

________________________________________________

*Continued on next page*  

# Martin Dies, Jr. State Park

☐ **CYPRESS SWAMP PADDLING TRAIL**     3.0 mi. · Moderate · 90 min.     Date:__________

This paddling route loops around the Wolf Creek Unit and Rush Creek Unit, where ducks often gather among cypress groves. Pull ashore to cast a line from the bank and try your luck at fishing.

Trail Notes: _________________________________________________

_____________________________________________________________

_____________________________________________________________

☐ **ACCESS TRAIL TO WMA HUNTING AREA**     0.1 mi.     Date:__________

Trail Notes: _________________________________________________

_____________________________________________________________

_____________________________________________________________

☐ **HWY-190 CONNECTING PATH**     0.3 mi.     Date:__________

Trail Notes: _________________________________________________

_____________________________________________________________

_____________________________________________________________

## 📍 Trailward Finds

☐ **OBSERVATION PIER**
DATE:

☐ **CYPRESS FOREST**
DATE:

☐ **WILDLIFE VIEWING STATION**
DATE:

☐ **NIGHT SKY LOOKOUT**
DATE:

☐ **SWAMP DECK**
DATE:

☐ **SUNSET VISTA**
DATE:

Park Website     Trail Map

Visit the Texas Parks & Wildlife
Department at tpwd.texas.gov

# Mission Tejas State Park

☐ KARL LOVETT TRAIL    0.5 mi. • Moderate • 30 min.    Date:__________

This moderately challenging route leads past several of the park's historic landmarks.

Trail Notes: ________________________________________________
________________________________________________
________________________________________________

☐ STEEP RAVINE TRAIL    2.4 mi. • Challenging • 90 min.    Date:__________

This demanding hike offers a great way to build endurance while exploring the park's more rugged landscapes.

Trail Notes: ________________________________________________
________________________________________________
________________________________________________

☐ HARDWOOD TRAIL    0.5 mi. • Moderate • 30 min.    Date:__________

This moderate hike passes through low-lying areas of the park known for their ecological diversity.

Trail Notes: ________________________________________________
________________________________________________
________________________________________________

☐ OLEN MATCHETT TRAIL    0.5 mi. • Challenging • 45 min.    Date:__________

This brief route is steep and challenging, climbing through forested highlands.

Trail Notes: ________________________________________________
________________________________________________
________________________________________________

☐ CCC BATHTUB TRAIL    0.1 mi. • Easy • 10 min.    Date:__________

This short outing leads to an intriguing rock formation worth a closer look.

Trail Notes: ________________________________________________
________________________________________________
________________________________________________

Continued on next page    

# Mission Tejas State Park

☐ **TEJAS TIMBER TRAIL**   0.5 mi. •   Easy   • 20 min.   Date:________

This easy loop circles the pond and passes several outdoor exhibits along the way.

Trail Notes: _______________________________________________

_______________________________________________

_______________________________________________


☐ **NABEDACHE LOOP**   1.1 mi. • Moderate • 45 min.   Date:________

This refreshing woodland walk follows a moderately easy route and passes remnants of the historic El Camino Real.

Trail Notes: _______________________________________________

_______________________________________________

_______________________________________________


☐ **CHIMNEY LOOP**   0.9 mi. • Challenging • 45 min.   Date:________

This demanding hike climbs rolling hills beneath a tall canopy of pine trees.

Trail Notes: _______________________________________________

_______________________________________________

_______________________________________________


☐ **BIG PINE TRAIL**   0.6 mi. • Challenging • 45 min.   Date:________

This challenging route weaves through the heart of the pine forest and links to several other trails.

Trail Notes: _______________________________________________

_______________________________________________

_______________________________________________


☐ **WECHES RUN**   0.4 mi. • Moderate • 20 min.   Date:________

This relatively short, moderate trail descends from piney uplands into the bottomland hardwoods along San Pedro Creek.

Trail Notes: _______________________________________________

_______________________________________________

_______________________________________________

# Mission Tejas State Park

☐ LIGHTNING TRAIL 0.2 mi. • Easy • 15 min. Date:__________

This easy trail winds through pine forest and passes one of the park's oldest pine trees.

Trail Notes: __________________________________________

________________________________________________________

________________________________________________________

☐ SAN PEDRO SPUR 0.2 mi. • Easy • 10 min. Date:__________

This easy walk provides a connection to the Nabedache Loop and passes remnants of the historic El Camino Real de los Tejas.

Trail Notes: __________________________________________

________________________________________________________

________________________________________________________

☐ PRIMITIVE LOOP 0.8 mi. • Easy • 35 min. Date:__________

This easy walk passes through a developing pine savanna and connects with the Hardwood Trail and the Steep Ravine Trail.

Trail Notes: __________________________________________

________________________________________________________

________________________________________________________

☐ EL CAMINO REAL Date:__________

Trail Notes: __________________________________________

________________________________________________________

________________________________________________________

☐ CHIMNEY LOOP REST AREA 0.1 mi. Date:__________

Trail Notes: __________________________________________

________________________________________________________

________________________________________________________

☐ CHIMNEY LOOP ACCESS TRAIL 0.1 mi. Date:__________

Trail Notes: __________________________________________

________________________________________________________

________________________________________________________

*Continued on next page* 

# Mission Tejas State Park

☐ SAN PEDRO CREEK ACCESS TRAIL  0.02 mi.  Date:__________

Trail Notes: __________________________________________
______________________________________________________
______________________________________________________

☐ CEMETERY HILL TRAIL  0.4 mi.  Date:__________

Trail Notes: __________________________________________
______________________________________________________
______________________________________________________

☐ BIRD BLIND TRAIL  0.1 mi.  Date:__________

Trail Notes: __________________________________________
______________________________________________________
______________________________________________________

☐ STEEP STEP TRAIL  0.2 mi.  Date:__________

Trail Notes: __________________________________________
______________________________________________________
______________________________________________________

☐ FIRE TOWER TRAIL  0.08 mi.  Date:__________

Trail Notes: __________________________________________
______________________________________________________

## 📍 Trailward Finds

☐ COMMEMORATIVE MISSION
DATE:

☐ RICE FAMILY LOG HOME
DATE:

☐ CCC BATHTUBS
DATE:

☐ EL CAMINO REAL
DATE:

☐ FIRE TOWER HILL
DATE:

☐ SENTRY PINE
DATE:

Park Website    Trail Map
Visit the Texas Parks & Wildlife
Department at tpwd.texas.gov

# Tyler State Park

☐ A LOOP  2.6 mi. • Moderate • 1.5 hrs.  Date:___________

This trail features changes in elevation and may include obstacles such as loose gravel along the way.

Trail Notes: ______________________________________________

______________________________________________

______________________________________________

☐ B LOOP  3.1 mi. • Moderate • 2 hrs.  Date:___________

Spanning more than three miles, this trail includes frequent elevation changes and offers a challenging yet scenic journey through the park's diverse forest landscapes.

Trail Notes: ______________________________________________

______________________________________________

______________________________________________

☐ BLACKJACK NATURE TRAIL (hiking only)  0.3 mi. •  Easy  • 20 min.  Date:___________

This short, level trail crosses a grassy savanna and is well suited for families or anyone looking for an easy walk.

Trail Notes: ______________________________________________

______________________________________________

______________________________________________

☐ C LOOP  1.5 mi. • Challenging • 1 hr.  Date:___________

Though brief, this trail presents a challenge and passes some of the park's largest pine trees.

Trail Notes: ______________________________________________

______________________________________________

______________________________________________

☐ D LOOP  2.2 mi. • Challenging • 1.5 hrs.  Date:___________

This trail passes through multiple forest habitats that draw a wide range of migratory birds. Bringing binoculars can enhance the birdwatching experience along the way.

Trail Notes: ______________________________________________

______________________________________________

______________________________________________

*Continued on next page*  

# Tyler State Park

☐ **EZ LOOP**  0.8 mi. • Easy • 45 min.  Date:__________

From this point, three different trails branch out, allowing hikers to choose a route that best matches their skill level.

Trail Notes: ______________________________________________

________________________________________________________

________________________________________________________

☐ **LAKESHORE TRAIL**  2.1 mi. • Easy • 1.5 hrs.  Date:__________
(hiking only)

This mostly level trail includes plenty of places to picnic, fish, or pause and enjoy the scenery. Portions of the route follow the main park road, so please stay aware of traffic and be mindful not to pass through occupied campsites.

Trail Notes: ______________________________________________

________________________________________________________

________________________________________________________

☐ **WHISPERING PINES TRAIL** (hiking only)  1.0 mi. • Moderate • 1.5 hrs.  Date:__________

This trail was developed more than 70 years ago by the Civilian Conservation Corps, who planted pine trees and constructed a wading pool along with a small waterfall.

Trail Notes: ______________________________________________

________________________________________________________

________________________________________________________

## ⦿ Trailward Finds

☐ **HISTORY LIVES HERE**
DATE:

☐ **CCC ROCK DAM**
DATE:

☐ **BIRD OBSERVATION BLIND**
DATE:

☐ **VIEW FROM THE PAST**
DATE:

☐ **CCC OVERLOOK**
DATE:

☐ **BEAVER POND**
DATE:

Park Website     Trail Map
Visit the Texas Parks & Wildlife
Department at tpwd.texas.gov

# Village Creek State Park

☐ BEECHWOOD TRAIL    0.1 mi. •    Easy      Date:_________

This connector route leads from the picnic area to the Loblolly Trail and the Water Oak Trail.

Trail Notes: _______________________________________________

_______________________________________________

_______________________________________________

☐ BIKE/FITNESS TRAIL    0.5 mi. • Moderate      Date:_________

This trail features fitness stations designed for stretching and strength-building along the route.

Trail Notes: _______________________________________________

_______________________________________________

_______________________________________________

☐ LIL' PAWS NATURE TRAIL    0.1 mi. •    Easy      Date:_________

Located beside the playground, this short trail is designed especially for kids.

Trail Notes: _______________________________________________

_______________________________________________

_______________________________________________

☐ LOBLOLLY TRAIL    0.1 mi. •    Easy      Date:_________

This short connector provides access from the main parking lot to the Water Oak Trail.

Trail Notes: _______________________________________________

_______________________________________________

_______________________________________________

☐ RIVER BIRCH TRAIL    0.2 mi. •    Easy      Date:_________

This spur trail links the Village Creek Trail with the Water Oak Trail, making it easy to explore more of the park.

Trail Notes: _______________________________________________

_______________________________________________

_______________________________________________

*Continued on next page*    

# Village Creek State Park

☐ **TUPELO TRAIL**        0.8 mi. • Moderate        Date:_________

Accessed from the Village Creek Trail, this route leaves the creekside and moves into bottomland forest and quiet backwater sloughs.

Trail Notes: _________________________________________________

_____________________________________________________________

_____________________________________________________________


☐ **VILLAGE CREEK TRAIL**        2.2 mi. • Challenging        Date:_________

This trail follows scenic Village Creek and leads to the park's well-known sandbar, a popular spot for picnicking or cooling off in the water.

Trail Notes: _________________________________________________

_____________________________________________________________

_____________________________________________________________


☐ **VILLAGE SLOUGH OUTER LOOP**        1.0 mi. • Moderate        Date:_________

This trail provides a quiet walk alongside Village Slough before curving into sandy terrain dotted with longleaf pines and native grasses.

Trail Notes: _________________________________________________

_____________________________________________________________

_____________________________________________________________


☐ **VILLAGE SLOUGH INNER LOOP**        0.5 mi. • Moderate        Date:_________

Reached from the Village Slough Outer Loop, this route offers a shorter walk along Village Slough.

Trail Notes: _________________________________________________

_____________________________________________________________

_____________________________________________________________


☐ **WATER OAK TRAIL**        2.4 mi. • Moderate        Date:_________

This trail showcases a wide range of plant life, from prickly pear cactus and yucca in the pine savanna to cypress and tupelo in the bottomland swamps.

Trail Notes: _________________________________________________

_____________________________________________________________

_____________________________________________________________

# Village Creek State Park

☐ LONGLEAF LOOP      0.9 mi. • Moderate      Date:_________

This newer trail provides an up-close look at a 37-acre longleaf pine savanna restoration currently underway.

Trail Notes: ________________________________________________

_____________________________________________________________

_____________________________________________________________

☐ YAUPON LOOP      0.9 mi. •    Easy      Date:_________

Accessed from the Water Oak Trail, this loop adds about a mile of scenic hiking through a mature longleaf pine savanna restoration area.

Trail Notes: ________________________________________________

_____________________________________________________________

_____________________________________________________________

## 📍 Trailward Finds

☐ CANOE LAUNCH
DATE:

☐ SAPSUCKER TREE
DATE:

☐ BEAVER SWAMP
DATE:

☐ LONGLEAF PINE SAVANNA RESTORATION
DATE:

Park Website      Trail Map

Visit the Texas Parks & Wildlife
Department at tpwd.texas.gov

# SOUTHEAST TEXAS

## REGION

| TRAILS TO EXPLORE | PARKS INCLUDED |
|---|---|
| 45 | 5 |

## Regional Milestones

☐ First Park Completed

Trail: _________________

Date: _________________

☐ Final Park Completed

Trail: _________________

Date: _________________

☐ Favorite Trail

Trail: _________________

Date: _________________

☐ Longest Trail Completed

Limestone Bluffs Paddling Trail

Date: _________________

☐ Shortest Trail Completed

Kinglet Trail

Date: _________________

☐ Most Challenging Trail Completed

Trail: _________________

Date: _________________

## All **45** Southeast Texas Trails Completed

67.38 Miles Hiked

Date: _________________     Total Miles Hiked: _________________

# Bastrop State Park

☐ PINEY HILL SPUR          0.3 mi.  •  Moderate                    Date:___________

Camping in Piney Hill? This trail provides a convenient connection to the rest of the park's trail network. About halfway along, exposed Carrizo sandstone can be seen—the same material used by the Civilian Conservation Corps to construct park features in the 1930s.

Trail Notes: ___________________________________________________

_______________________________________________________________

_______________________________________________________________

☐ PINE WARBLER TRAIL  0.3 mi.  •  Moderate                    Date:___________

Starting near the playground, this trail winds through native grasses and heads toward the Scenic Overlook Trail and the Post Oak Spur. Sandy areas near Copperas Creek are good spots to look for animal tracks.

Trail Notes: ___________________________________________________

_______________________________________________________________

_______________________________________________________________

☐ POST OAK SPUR          0.5 mi.  •  Moderate                    Date:___________

This route begins beneath shady post oaks before climbing into a hilly, rocky stretch. Connecting with the Pine Warbler Trail leads onward to the Refectory.

Trail Notes: ___________________________________________________

_______________________________________________________________

_______________________________________________________________

☐ FARKLEBERRY SPUR    0.4 mi.  •  Moderate                    Date:___________

This gently graded route connects with the Scenic Overlook Trail and is well suited for beginners. Early morning is a great time to watch for bird activity along the way.

Trail Notes: ___________________________________________________

_______________________________________________________________

_______________________________________________________________

☐ SCENIC OVERLOOK TRAIL          1.7 mi.  •  Moderate                    Date:___________

A steep descent from the overlook leads into the inner loop near Copperas Creek, passing a historic CCC-built hike-in picnic site.

Trail Notes: ___________________________________________________

_______________________________________________________________

_______________________________________________________________

# Bastrop State Park

☐ LOST PINES LOOP     8.4 mi. • Challenging     Date:________

As the park's longest backcountry route, this trail crosses a wide range of terrain, from steep climbs to gentler downhill stretches. Be sure to carry plenty of water, snacks, and sunscreen. Harmon Road or the nearby power line can be used as landmarks or to help create a loop (additional mileage not included).

Trail Notes: __________________________________________________

____________________________________________________________

____________________________________________________________

☐ HERON HIDEAWAY     1.4 mi. • Moderate     Date:________

This rocky footpath circles the 20-acre Little Alum Creek Lake, offering excellent opportunities for fishing, birdwatching, and wildlife viewing. Access is by foot only, and camping is not permitted in this area.

Trail Notes: __________________________________________________

____________________________________________________________

____________________________________________________________

☐ TREE ARMY TRAILS     Up to 4.5 mi. • Easy     Date:________

North of the park road, the hilly trails wind through stands of loblolly pine and offer scenic park views, with slopes and curves that can be challenging for all users. South of the road, trails circle Lake Mina, a popular spot for family fishing. These south-side routes are wheelchair accessible and stroller friendly. All Tree Army Trails are open to both hikers and cyclists. The trails listed below are included in the TREE ARMY TRAILS.

Trail Notes: __________________________________________________

____________________________________________________________

____________________________________________________________

☐ THE OL' 9 LOOP     1.5 mi.     Date:________

Trail Notes: __________________________________________________

____________________________________________________________

____________________________________________________________

☐ LAKE MINA LOOP     0.8 mi.     Date:________

Trail Notes: __________________________________________________

____________________________________________________________

____________________________________________________________

*Continued on next page*     

# Bastrop State Park

☐ CARPENTER CROSSOVER     0.3 mi.     Date:_________

Trail Notes: _______________________________

_______________________________

_______________________________

☐ CO. 1805     1.0 mi.     Date:_________

Trail Notes: _______________________________

_______________________________

_______________________________

☐ PLAYFIELD PATH     0.1 mi.     Date:_________

Trail Notes: _______________________________

_______________________________

_______________________________

☐ BLACKSMITH SPUR     0.3 mi.     Date:_________

Trail Notes: _______________________________

_______________________________

_______________________________

☐ STONEMASON COURSE     0.4 mi.     Date:_________

Trail Notes: _______________________________

_______________________________

_______________________________

☐ CO. 1811     0.3 mi.     Date:_________

Trail Notes: _______________________________

_______________________________

_______________________________

☐ OLD ROAD BED     1.0 mi.     Date:_________

Trail Notes: _______________________________

_______________________________

_______________________________

# Bastrop State Park

☐ **FEHR'S OVERLOOK TRACE**   1.0 mi.   Date:_________

Trail Notes: _______________________________________________

_______________________________________________

_______________________________________________

☐ **POST OAK SPUR**   0.5 mi.   Date:_________

Trail Notes: _______________________________________________

_______________________________________________

_______________________________________________

☐ **LAKE SPUR TRAIL**   0.2 mi.   Date:_________

Trail Notes: _______________________________________________

_______________________________________________

_______________________________________________

## 📍 Trailward Finds

☐ **LAKE MINA**
DATE:

☐ **HISTORIC GOLF SHELTER**
DATE:

☐ **REFECTORY**
DATE:

☐ **SCENIC OVERLOOK**
DATE:

☐ **NATURE'S HANDIWORK**
DATE:

☐ **BRACKEN FERNS**
DATE:

☐ **FEHR'S OVERLOOK**
DATE:

☐ **HISTORIC WATER FOUNTAIN**
DATE:

☐ **HISTORIC WATER FOUNTAIN**
DATE:

**Park Website**   **Trail Map**

Visit the Texas Parks & Wildlife
Department at tpwd.texas.gov

# Buescher State Park

☐ **WINDING WOODLAND TRAIL**  1.5 mi. (one way) • Moderate • 1.5 hrs.  Date:_________

A canopy of oak and cedar trees shelters this winding forest route.

Trail Notes: ________________________________________________

________________________________________________

________________________________________________

☐ **PINE GULCH TRAIL**  4.0 mi. (round trip) • Challenging • 2 hrs.  Date:_________

Towering loblolly pines cover the steep slopes of Pine Gulch, an area still showing signs of the 2015 Hidden Pines wildfire.

Trail Notes: ________________________________________________

________________________________________________

________________________________________________

☐ **ROOSEVELT'S CUTOFF**  0.5 mi. (one way) • Moderate • 30 min.  Date:_________

A shaded creek corridor defines this trail, named in honor of the president who launched the Civilian Conservation Corps.

Trail Notes: ________________________________________________

________________________________________________

________________________________________________

☐ **BARRED OWL PATH**  0.1 mi. • Easy • 10 min.  Date:_________

Looking to modify your route? This short connector joins opposite sides of the Pine Gulch Trail.

Trail Notes: ________________________________________________

________________________________________________

________________________________________________

☐ **CCC CROSSOVER**  0.1 mi. • Easy • 10 min.  Date:_________

This short walk reveals carefully built stonework, staircases, and a historic bridge created during the Civilian Conservation Corps era.

Trail Notes: ________________________________________________

________________________________________________

________________________________________________

# Buescher State Park



☐ BIG TREE RETREAT     0.03 mi. •     Easy     • 5 min.     Date:_________

This is a peaceful place to stop, shaded by an impressive cedar elm tree.

Trail Notes: ______________________________________________

______________________________________________

______________________________________________

## 📍 Trailward Finds

☐ CCC CROSSOVER
DATE:

☐ BIG TREE RETREAT
DATE:

☐ FLOWER VIEW CROSSING
DATE:

☐ SCENIC OVERLOOK
DATE:

☐ SCENIC OVERLOOK
DATE:

☐ PINE GULCH
DATE:

Park Website     Trail Map

Visit the Texas Parks & Wildlife
Department at tpwd.texas.gov

# Fort Parker State Park

☐ **BUR OAK TRAIL**  0.5 mi. • Easy • 20 min.  Date:________
(loop)

Ideal for families, this loop winds through lakeside woods near Fort Parker Lake and includes a wildlife blind overlooking a heron rookery. Pick up a Bur Oak Trail guide at park headquarters before heading out.

Trail Notes: ________________________________________

________________________________________

________________________________________

☐ **SPRINGFIELD TRAIL**  1.8 mi. • Easy • 45 min.  Date:________
(loop)

Traces of the past shape this loop as it winds through forest, prairie openings, and the old Springfield town site, with opportunities to explore a historic cemetery or fish at Lake Springfield.

Trail Notes: ________________________________________

________________________________________

________________________________________

☐ **NAVASOTA RIVER TRAIL**  1.9 mi. • Easy • 45 min.  Date:________
(one way)

Serving as a key connector, this shaded trail runs along the north shore, tying together campground areas and continuing on to the Navasota River, with a convenient launch for the Limestone Bluffs Paddling Trail.

Trail Notes: ________________________________________

________________________________________

________________________________________

☐ **RIVER LOOP**  0.9 mi. • Easy  Date:________
(one way)

Branching off the Navasota River Trail, this gentle route follows the river's edge beneath a canopy of shade, offering an easy and enjoyable walk through the woods.

Trail Notes: ________________________________________

________________________________________

________________________________________

☐ **BAINES CREEK TRAIL**  2.5 mi. • Moderate • 2 hrs.  Date:________
(one way)

An easy stretch along Polecat Slough opens this trail, followed by a steady climb that leads to a scenic overlook well worth the effort. Access to the route is available from the satellite park.

Trail Notes: ________________________________________

________________________________________

________________________________________

# Fort Parker State Park

☐ **LIMESTONE BLUFFS PADDLING TRAIL**  10.8 mi. *(round trip)* • Easy • 6 hrs.  Date:____________

A calm paddle along the Navasota River offers a close look at the lush river corridor between Fort Parker State Park and the Confederate Reunion Grounds State Historic Site. Canoe and kayak rentals may be available—check with the park office before heading out.

Trail Notes: _______________________________________________

_______________________________________________

_______________________________________________

## ◉ Trailward Finds

☐ **LIMESTONE BLUFFS**
DATE:

☐ **SPRINGFIELD CEMETERY**
DATE:

☐ **RECREATION HALL / NATURE CENTER**
DATE:

☐ **PARK HEADQUARTERS**
DATE:

☐ **LAKE SPRINGFIELD**
DATE:

☐ **FORT PARKER DAM**
DATE:

☐ **HERON ROOKERY**
DATE:

☐ **BAINES CREEK TRAIL OVERLOOK**
DATE:

Park Website        Trail Map

Visit the Texas Parks & Wildlife
Department at tpwd.texas.gov

# Huntsville State Park

☐ **TRIPLE C TRAIL**     8.4 mi. • Challenging          Date:_________
(round trip)

This remote route is ideal for hikers seeking a wide range of ecosystems in a quieter setting. Along the way, remnants of work completed by the Civilian Conservation Corps highlight the park's historical legacy.

Trail Notes: _______________________________________________
_______________________________________________
_______________________________________________

☐ **CHINQUAPIN TRAIL**     6.9 mi. • Challenging          Date:_________
(round trip)

Circling the lake from start to finish, this route offers the most complete view of the park. The path crosses marshy areas rich with wildlife, where shorebirds are common and nutria are often spotted.

Trail Notes: _______________________________________________
_______________________________________________
_______________________________________________

☐ **DOGWOOD TRAIL**     1.8 mi. • Moderate          Date:_________

This trail takes its name from the dogwood, a common understory tree in the area. In spring, dogwoods stand out with bright white, petal-like bracts that signal the season's arrival.

Trail Notes: _______________________________________________
_______________________________________________
_______________________________________________

☐ **PRAIRIE BRANCH LOOP**     1.5 mi. • Moderate          Date:_________
(round trip)

This compact loop showcases contrasting landscapes, with one section following the shoreline of Lake Raven and the other passing through a forest of mixed pine and hardwoods.

Trail Notes: _______________________________________________
_______________________________________________
_______________________________________________

☐ **COLONEH TRAIL**     0.8 mi. • Easy          Date:_________

This short trail commemorates one of Huntsville's best-known figures, Sam Houston. He was given the name "Coloneh," meaning raven, by Cherokee leader Oolooteka—the inspiration behind the trail's name.

Trail Notes: _______________________________________________
_______________________________________________
_______________________________________________

# Huntsville State Park

☐ LOBLOLLY TRAIL          0.2 mi.   •     Easy                    Date:___________
(round trip)

This brief loop starts and finishes at the nature center and takes its name
from the dominant pine species found throughout the park.

Trail Notes: _______________________________________________

______________________________________________________________

______________________________________________________________


☐ TRIPLE C CUTOFF          0.6 mi.                              Date:___________

Trail Notes: _______________________________________________

______________________________________________________________

______________________________________________________________


# 📍 Trailward Finds

☐ HISTORIC DAM AND SPILLWAY
DATE:

☐ HEADWATER BOARDWALKS
DATE:

☐ CCC CULVERTS
DATE:

☐ CCC LODGE
DATE:

☐ BIRD BLIND
DATE:

☐ FLATWATER PONDS
DATE:

Park Website          Trail Map

Visit the Texas Parks & Wildlife
Department at tpwd.texas.gov

# Sheldon Lake State Park

☐ POND LOOP TRAIL    0.6 mi. •   Easy   •   30 – 60 min.   Date:_________

Once used for fish production, 28 ponds now form an important wetland habitat that lines this short, half-mile route.

Trail Notes: _________________________________________________

_____________________________________________________________

_____________________________________________________________

☐ PRAIRIE TRAIL    0.6 mi.            Date:_________

☐ WETLAND LOOP    0.2 mi. •   Easy   •   30 – 60 min.

Restored tall-grass prairie and seasonal wetlands define these trails, which can be reached from the prairie parking lot or the Swamp Rabbit Trail.

Trail Notes: _________________________________________________

_____________________________________________________________

_____________________________________________________________

☐ SWAMP RABBIT TRAIL    0.4 mi. •   Easy   •   15 min.   Date:_________

An overhead canopy that shifts with the seasons shades this walk, where the rhythmic tapping of woodpeckers is often heard among the trees.

Trail Notes: _________________________________________________

_____________________________________________________________

_____________________________________________________________

☐ BENT PINE TRAIL    0.2 mi. •   Easy   •   10 min.   Date:_________

Encircled by pine shade, this loop passes around a former hatchery pond that now reflects how the landscape has adapted and renewed itself over time.

Trail Notes: _________________________________________________

_____________________________________________________________

_____________________________________________________________

☐ ARMADILLO TRAIL    0.08 mi. •   Easy   •   5 min.   Date:_________

A shaded woodland corridor connects the Pond Loop with the Swamp Rabbit Trail.

Trail Notes: _________________________________________________

_____________________________________________________________

_____________________________________________________________

# Sheldon Lake State Park

☐ KINGLET TRAIL     0.07 mi. •   Easy   •   5 min.    Date:________

This route cuts across a dry pond, providing a direct link between the Swamp Rabbit Trail and the Pond Loop Trail.

Trail Notes: ____________________________________________________________________________________________________________________________

# 📍 Trailward Finds

☐ **POND CROSSING**
DATE:

☐ **JOHN JACOB OBSERVATION TOWER**
DATE:

☐ **WILDLIFE VIEWING PLATFORM**
DATE:

☐ **AQUATIC LAB 1**
DATE:

☐ **FISHING DECK**
DATE:

☐ **POND PAVILION**
DATE:

**Park Website**      **Trail Map**

Visit the Texas Parks & Wildlife
Department at tpwd.texas.gov

# SOUTH TEXAS

## REGION

**TRAILS TO EXPLORE**

61

**PARKS INCLUDED**

9

## Regional Milestones

☐ First Park Completed

Trail: _______________

Date: _______________

☐ Final Park Completed

Trail: _______________

Date: _______________

☐ Favorite Trail

Trail: _______________

Date: _______________

☐ Longest Trail Completed

Old Park Roads

Date: _______________

☐ Shortest Trail Completed

Trail: _______________

Date: _______________

☐ Most Challenging Trail Completed

Trail: _______________

Date: _______________

## —— All **61** South Texas Trails Completed ——

38.94 Miles Hiked

Date: _______________          Total Miles Hiked: _______________

# Bentsen–Rio Grande Valley State Park

☐ **OLD PARK ROADS**      3.8 mi. •      Easy      •   2 hrs.      Date:___________
(all roads combined)

Several former park roads—now closed to vehicle traffic—offer wide, accessible routes for exploring the park at an easy pace. These include Park Rd 43, Kingfisher Corridor, Acacia Loop, Roadrunner Crossing, Mesquite Lane, and Pauraque Way. For a more relaxed outing, ask about the park's tram schedule.

Trail Notes: _________________________________________________

_______________________________________________________________

_______________________________________________________________


☐ **RESACA VIEJA TRAIL**    1.3 mi. •    Easy to    • 45 min. to   Date:___________
Moderate       1 hr.

One of the park's most botanically varied areas lies along this route, where a rich mix of plant life supports an equally diverse range of wildlife—so stay alert for animal activity along the way.

Trail Notes: _________________________________________________

_______________________________________________________________

_______________________________________________________________


☐ **GREEN JAY TRAIL**      0.3 mi. •      Easy      • 20 min.    Date:___________

Along the resaca's edge, the banks offer shelter for a variety of wildlife, while nearby open areas make it easier to spot species such as wild turkeys.

Trail Notes: _________________________________________________

_______________________________________________________________

_______________________________________________________________


☐ **KISKADEE TRAIL**      0.3 mi. •      Easy      • 20 min.    Date:___________

This route explores the former campground area, looping around Acacia Loop and passing features worth a closer look, including a bird blind and nearby water features.

Trail Notes: _________________________________________________

_______________________________________________________________

_______________________________________________________________

# Bentsen–Rio Grande Valley State Park

☐ RIO GRANDE TRAIL    1.7 mi.  •  Easy to Moderate  •  1 hr.    Date:_________

As the park's longest route, this trail offers a quiet, backcountry feel. A stop at the Hawk Tower rewards hikers with sweeping views before the path slips into a secluded forest rarely traveled by visitors.

Trail Notes: ______________________________________________

______________________________________________

______________________________________________

## ⚲ Trailward Finds

☐ **HEADQUARTERS GARDENS**
DATE:

☐ **NATURE CENTER**
DATE:

☐ **EBONY GROVE**
DATE:

☐ **KINGFISHER OVERLOOK**
DATE:

☐ **HAWK TOWER**
DATE:

Park Website     Trail Map

Visit the Texas Parks & Wildlife Department at tpwd.texas.gov

# Choke Canyon State Park

No official **trail map** is available for this park. Use the space below to record your hike time and difficulty.

☐ NATURE TRAIL  .6 mi. •  •  Date:__________

Trail Notes: _______________________________________

_______________________________________

_______________________________________

☐ NATURE TRAIL  .2 mi. •  •  Date:__________

Trail Notes: _______________________________________

_______________________________________

_______________________________________

☐ BIRD TRAIL  .5 mi. •  •  Date:__________

Trail Notes: _______________________________________

_______________________________________

_______________________________________

☐ NATURE TRAIL  .4 mi. •  •  Date:__________

Trail Notes: _______________________________________

_______________________________________

_______________________________________

☐ NATURE TRAIL  .7 mi. •  •  Date:__________

Trail Notes: _______________________________________

_______________________________________

_______________________________________

## Trailward Finds

☐ FISH CLEANING
DATE:

☐ SCENIC OVERLOOK
DATE:

☐ BASKETBALL COURT
DATE:

☐ TENNIS COURT
DATE:

☐ BASEBALL FIELD
DATE:

Park Website  Park Map

Visit the Texas Parks & Wildlife
Department at tpwd.texas.gov

# Estero Llano Grande State Park

☐ **ALLIGATOR LAKE TRAIL**    0.1 mi. •   Easy   •   15 min.    Date:________

Beginning along the south fork of the Camino de Aves, this route leads to Alligator Lake, where resident American alligators and wading birds such as herons and egrets are often seen.

Trail Notes: ________________________________________

________________________________________

________________________________________

☐ **LLANO GRANDE HIKING TRAIL**    1.46 mi. •   Easy   •   1 hr.    Date:________

Elevated above the surrounding wetlands, this levee forms part of the Rio Grande floodway and looks out over Llano Grande Lake, a natural lake within the Arroyo Colorado system. The open views make this a good place to watch for roseate spoonbills and white-tailed kites. Access is available from the Wader's Trail, Camino de Aves, or Orchard Trail.

Trail Notes: ________________________________________

________________________________________

________________________________________

☐ **WADER'S TRAIL**    1.16 mi. •   Easy   •   1 hr.    Date:________

These routes pass through the park's primary wetland zones, where water and food sources draw a wide range of birds and wildlife. The surrounding brush and grasslands were once cultivated fields, now reclaimed by nature.

Trail Notes: ________________________________________

________________________________________

________________________________________

☐ **CAMINO DE AVES**    .94 mi. •   Easy   •   1 hr.    Date:________

This drier section of the park supports plants adapted to arid conditions, including honey mesquite, prickly pear cactus, and amargosa shrubs. Access begins near the northeastern end of the Wader's Trail.

Trail Notes: ________________________________________

________________________________________

________________________________________

*Continued on next page*    

# Estero Llano Grande State Park

☐ ORCHARD TRAIL · .42 mi. · Easy · 30 min. · Date:_________

Reaching this route from either the Camino de Aves or the Llano Grande Hiking Trail brings you beneath broad honey mesquite canopies. These mature trees make the Orchard Trail a reliable spot for observing migrating bird species.

Trail Notes: _______________________________________________

_______________________________________________

_______________________________________________

☐ TROPICAL AREA TRAILS · 0.74 mi. · Easy · 1 hr. · Date:_________

Once home to Lakeview RV Park, this area now features a network of paved paths shaded by a dense mix of native brush and introduced trees, creating excellent habitat for both resident and migratory birds. For a change of scenery, step off the pavement onto the Green Jay Trail to experience a pocket of distinctive old-growth habitat. The Trails below are part of the Tropical Area Trails

Trail Notes: _______________________________________________

_______________________________________________

_______________________________________________

☐ POWERLINE TRAIL · 0.2 mi. · Date:_________

Trail Notes: _______________________________________________

_______________________________________________

_______________________________________________

☐ SPOONBILL TRAIL · 0.5 mi. · Date:_________

Trail Notes: _______________________________________________

_______________________________________________

_______________________________________________

☐ SCISSORTAIL LOOP · 0.07 mi. · Date:_________

Trail Notes: _______________________________________________

_______________________________________________

_______________________________________________

# Estero Llano Grande State Park

☐ FLYCATCHER          0.05 mi.                    Date:___________

Trail Notes: ___________________________________________
_______________________________________________________
_______________________________________________________

☐ ALOHA DRIVE          0.12 mi.                    Date:___________

Trail Notes: ___________________________________________
_______________________________________________________
_______________________________________________________

☐ GREEN JAY NATURE
   TRAIL                0.18 mi.                    Date:___________

Trail Notes: ___________________________________________
_______________________________________________________
_______________________________________________________

☐ TROGON ALLEY         0.1 mi.                     Date:___________

Trail Notes: ___________________________________________
_______________________________________________________
_______________________________________________________

☐ KINGBIRD TRAIL       0.11 mi.                    Date:___________

Trail Notes: ___________________________________________
_______________________________________________________
_______________________________________________________

☐ BECARD TRAIL         0.05 mi.                    Date:___________

Trail Notes: ___________________________________________
_______________________________________________________
_______________________________________________________

☐ TYRANNULET TRAIL  0.13 mi.                       Date:___________

Trail Notes: ___________________________________________
_______________________________________________________
_______________________________________________________

*Continued on next page*    

# Estero Llano Grande State Park

☐ HOOT HOOT TRAIL          0.17 mi.                    Date:__________

Trail Notes: _______________________________________________

_______________________________________________

_______________________________________________

☐ ENTRANCE WALKWAY          0.07 mi.                    Date:__________

Trail Notes: _______________________________________________

_______________________________________________

_______________________________________________

☐ CAMP THICKET TRAIL          0.16 mi.                    Date:__________

Trail Notes: _______________________________________________

_______________________________________________

_______________________________________________

## ● Trailward Finds

☐ **ALLIGATOR LAKE**
DATE:

☐ **INDIGO BLIND**
DATE:

☐ **GREEN JAY TRAIL**
DATE:

☐ **LLANO GRANDE LAKE**
DATE:

Park Website          Trail Map

Visit the Texas Parks & Wildlife
Department at tpwd.texas.gov

# Falcon State Park

No official **trail map** is available for this park. Use the space below to record your hike mileage, time and difficulty.
**Hiking trail is a loop = 2.6 miles total**

☐ DESERT TRAIL  •  •  Date:__________

Trail Notes: ______________________________________

____________________________________________________

☐ VERDIN TRAIL  •  •  Date:__________

Trail Notes: ______________________________________

____________________________________________________

☐ ROADRUNNER TRAIL  •  •  Date:__________

Trail Notes: ______________________________________

____________________________________________________

☐ WHITEBRUSH TRAIL  •  •  Date:__________

Trail Notes: ______________________________________

____________________________________________________

☐ WOODLANDS TRAILS  •  •  Date:__________

Trail Notes: ______________________________________

____________________________________________________

# Trailward Finds

☐ FISH CLEANING
DATE:

☐ BUTTERFLY GARDEN
DATE:

☐ WILDLIFE VIEWING
DATE:

☐ BOAT RAMP
DATE:

Park Website  Park Map

Visit the Texas Parks & Wildlife
Department at tpwd.texas.gov

# Goliad State Park & Historic Site

No official **trail map** is available for this park. Use the space below to record your hike time and difficulty.

☐ **SAN ANTONIO RIVER TRAIL**   1.0 mi.  •   •   Date:__________

Trail Notes: _______________________________

_______________________________

_______________________________

☐ **ARANAMA TRAIL**   .25 mi.  •   •   Date:__________

Trail Notes: _______________________________

_______________________________

_______________________________

☐ **ANGEL OF GOLIAD**
(hike and bike trail)   2.5 mi.  •   •   Date:__________

Trail Notes: _______________________________

_______________________________

_______________________________

☐ **STRIPLING'S STROLL**   •   •   Date:__________

Trail Notes: _______________________________

_______________________________

_______________________________

## ⦿ Trailward Finds

☐ **MISSION ROSARIO**
DATE:

☐ **CARDINAL'S HAVEN BLIND**
DATE:

☐ **MISSION ESPÍRITU SANTO**
DATE:

☐ **BIRTHPLACE OF GENERAL IGNACIO ZARAGOZA**
DATE:

☐ **EL CAMINO REAL DE LOS TEJAS VISITOR CENTER**
DATE:

Park Website    Park Map

Visit the Texas Parks & Wildlife
Department at tpwd.texas.gov

# Lake Casa Blanca International State Park

☐ ROADRUNNER TRAIL   1.0 mi. •   Easy   • 30 min.   Date:_________

A smooth path across the Lake Casa Blanca Dam makes for an easy walk or bike ride. Visiting near dusk offers a memorable bonus, when Mexican free-tailed bats emerge from beneath the bridge along the Bob Bullock Loop.

Trail Notes: _______________________________________________

_______________________________________________

_______________________________________________

☐ MESQUITE BEND TRAIL   1.5 mi. •   Easy – Moderate   • 1.5 hrs.   Date:_________

A series of switchbacks adds a solid climb on this route, bringing hikers close to the mesquite trees that give the trail its name. Shaded areas along the way are good places to spot jackrabbits or white-tailed deer resting out of the sun.

Trail Notes: _______________________________________________

_______________________________________________

_______________________________________________

☐ OSPREY HILL LOOP   0.8 mi. • Moderate • 30 min.   Date:_________

A narrow singletrack climb leads to the top of an earthen water tank, where wide views open across the surrounding landscape. Loose footing and steep grades add a moderate challenge for mountain bikers. Overhead, osprey are sometimes seen passing by with fish from the lake.

Trail Notes: _______________________________________________

_______________________________________________

_______________________________________________

☐ WHITE-TAIL LOOP   1.0 mi. •   Easy   • 30 min.   Date:_________

Encircling the spillway, this loop can be traveled on foot or by bike and passes through open grasslands favored by species like savannah sparrows. Trees along the outer edge provide cover for animals such as javelina.

Trail Notes: _______________________________________________

_______________________________________________

_______________________________________________

# Lake Casa Blanca International State Park

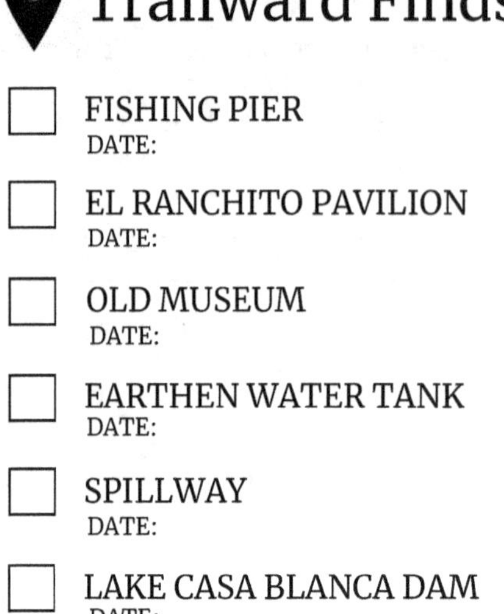

## Trailward Finds

- ☐ **FISHING PIER**
  DATE:

- ☐ **EL RANCHITO PAVILION**
  DATE:

- ☐ **OLD MUSEUM**
  DATE:

- ☐ **EARTHEN WATER TANK**
  DATE:

- ☐ **SPILLWAY**
  DATE:

- ☐ **LAKE CASA BLANCA DAM**
  DATE:

Park Website    Trail Map

Visit the Texas Parks & Wildlife
Department at tpwd.texas.gov

# Lake Corpus Christi State Park

No official **trail map** is available for this park. Use the space below to record your hike mileage, time and difficulty.

☐ CATFISH POINT TRAIL   •  •   Date:__________

Trail Notes: _______________________________________________

___________________________________________________________

___________________________________________________________

☐ LONGHORN TRAIL   •  •   Date:__________

Trail Notes: _______________________________________________

___________________________________________________________

___________________________________________________________

☐ KISKADEE TRAIL   •  •   Date:__________

Trail Notes: _______________________________________________

___________________________________________________________

___________________________________________________________

## 📍 Trailward Finds

☐ BIRD'S NEST SHELTER AREA
DATE:

☐ SCENIC OVERLOOK
DATE:

☐ CCC REFECTORY
DATE:

☐ BIRDING AREA
DATE:

☐ NATURE PLAYSCAPE
DATE:

☐ LAKE CORPUS CHRISTI
DATE:

Park Website     Park Map

Visit the Texas Parks & Wildlife
Department at tpwd.texas.gov

# Mustang Island State Park

No official **trails or trail map** is available for this park. Please add other important park finds.

## 📍 Trailward Finds

- ☐ **GULF OF MEXICO**
  DATE:

- ☐ **CORPUS CHRISTI BAY**
  DATE:

- ☐
  DATE:

**Park Website**     **Park Map**

Visit the Texas Parks & Wildlife
Department at tpwd.texas.gov

Park Notes: _______________________________________

_____________________________________________________

_____________________________________________________

_____________________________________________________

_____________________________________________________

_____________________________________________________

# Resaca de la Palma State Park

☐ EBONY TRAIL      0.2 mi. •    Easy    • 10 min.    Date:_________

Located nearest the Visitor Center, this gently curving trail moves through mature ebony–anacua woodland. An observation deck and boardwalk mark the far end of the route, with interpretive plant signage placed throughout. The trailhead begins behind the Visitor Center.

Trail Notes: _____________________________________________

___________________________________________________________

___________________________________________________________

☐ MESQUITE TRAIL      0.6 mi. • Moderate • 40 min.    Date:_________

This route winds through Tamaulipan thornscrub and restored grassland savanna, beginning at a trailhead located off the tram loop.

Trail Notes: _____________________________________________

___________________________________________________________

___________________________________________________________

☐ MEXICAN OLIVE TRAIL      0.3 mi. •    Easy    • 10 min.    Date:_________

Designed for accessibility, this ADA-compliant route is reserved for foot traffic only—bicycles are not permitted. The path leads to Observation Deck C and begins from a trailhead along the tram loop.

Trail Notes: _____________________________________________

___________________________________________________________

___________________________________________________________

☐ NORTH MEXICAN OLIVE TRAIL      0.4 mi. •    Easy    • 10 min.    Date:_________

Passing through a landscape dominated by tepeguaje and mesquite, this route links directly with the Mesquite Trail and the Mexican Olive Trail.

Trail Notes: _____________________________________________

___________________________________________________________

___________________________________________________________

☐ KISKADEE TRAIL      0.06 mi. •    Easy    • 5 min.    Date:_________

Dense stands of sugar hackberry and ebony frame this route as it leads toward Observation Deck A. The trailhead is located off the tram loop.

Trail Notes: _____________________________________________

___________________________________________________________

___________________________________________________________

*Continued on next page*    

# Resaca de la Palma State Park

☐ **FLYCATCHER TRAIL**    1.2 mi.  •  Moderate  •  40 min.    Date:________

This loop winds through a mix of thornscrub and savanna habitat, with access from the tram loop.

Trail Notes: ________________________________________________

________________________________________________

________________________________________________

☐ **HOG TRAIL**    0.2 mi.  •  Moderate  •  10 min.    Date:________

This connector provides access to Observation Deck D from the Flycatcher Trail.

Trail Notes: ________________________________________________

________________________________________________

________________________________________________

☐ **COYOTE TRAIL**    0.4 mi.  •  Moderate  •  15 min.    Date:________

This route twists through ebony and mesquite woodland, featuring narrow turns along the way.

Trail Notes: ________________________________________________

________________________________________________

________________________________________________

☐ **HUNTER'S LANE**    0.7 mi.  •  Moderate  •  35 min.    Date:________

This trail serves as a gateway to the park's more remote southern areas, providing access to Screwbean Alley as well as the Quail, White-winged Dove, and Yellowthroat loops.

Trail Notes: ________________________________________________

________________________________________________

________________________________________________

☐ **QUAIL LOOP**    1.3 mi.  •  Moderate  •  45 min.    Date:________

Grassland scenery defines this recommended biking loop, which opens up northeast-facing views of the Brownsville reservoir. The open landscape also makes this a good route for spotting osprey and other birds of prey.

Trail Notes: ________________________________________________

________________________________________________

________________________________________________

# Resaca de la Palma State Park

☐ **YELLOWTHROAT LOOP**    1.2 mi.    •    Easy    •    45 min.    Date:______________

This route passes through multiple habitat types, making it a strong choice for observing a wide range of wildlife.

Trail Notes: ____________________________________________

________________________________________________________

________________________________________________________

☐ **BOBCAT LANE**    1.3 mi.    •    Easy    •    45 min.    Date:______________

This route is well suited for biking and follows the park's western boundary along a levee via the Bobcat Trail.

Trail Notes: ____________________________________________

________________________________________________________

________________________________________________________

☐ **TRAM LOOP**    2.8 mi.    •    Easy    •    50 min.    Date:______________

This paved loop offers an easy route across the park, crossing two bridges with scenic views and seven access points along the way.

Trail Notes: ____________________________________________

________________________________________________________

________________________________________________________

☐ **SCREWBEAN ALLEY TRAIL**    0.2 mi.    Date:______________

Trail Notes: ____________________________________________

________________________________________________________

________________________________________________________

☐ **WHITE-WINGED DOVE LOOP**    0.9 mi.    Date:______________

Trail Notes: ____________________________________________

________________________________________________________

________________________________________________________

# Trailward Finds

☐ **EBONY TRAIL**
DATE:

☐ **2ND BRIDGE**
DATE:

☐ **HUNTER'S LANE**
DATE:

Park Website          Trail Map

Visit the Texas Parks & Wildlife
Department at tpwd.texas.gov

# CENTRAL TEXAS

## REGION

| TRAILS TO EXPLORE | PARKS INCLUDED |
|---|---|
| 221 | 21 |

## — Regional Milestones —

☐ First Park Completed

Trail: _______________

Date: _______________

☐ Final Park Completed

Trail: _______________

Date: _______________

☐ Favorite Trail

Trail: _______________

Date: _______________

☐ Longest Trail Completed

Lake Somerville Trailway

Date: _______________

☐ Shortest Trail Completed

Pump House Trail

Date: _______________

☐ Most Challenging Trail Completed

Trail: _______________

Date: _______________

## —— All **221** Central Texas Trails Completed ——

254.92 Miles Hiked

Date: _______________     Total Miles Hiked: _______________

# Albert & Bessie Kronkosky State Natural Area

This is a NEW Texas State Park that is not yet open.
Use this page to document trail names, mileage, time, and difficulty once maps and trails are released.

☐    •    •    Date:________

Trail Notes: ________________________________
_____________________________________________
_____________________________________________
_____________________________________________

☐    •    •    Date:________

Trail Notes: ________________________________
_____________________________________________
_____________________________________________
_____________________________________________

☐    •    •    Date:________

Trail Notes: ________________________________
_____________________________________________
_____________________________________________
_____________________________________________

☐    •    •    Date:________

Trail Notes: ________________________________
_____________________________________________
_____________________________________________
_____________________________________________

## Trailward Finds

☐ DATE:

☐ DATE:

☐ DATE:

☐ DATE:

☐ DATE:

### Park Website

Visit the Texas Parks & Wildlife
Department at tpwd.texas.gov

# Bear Creek State Park

This is a NEW Texas State Park that is not yet open.
Use this page to document trail names, mileage, time, and difficulty once maps and trails are released.

☐ • • Date:__________

Trail Notes: _______________________________________________

_______________________________________________

_______________________________________________

_______________________________________________

☐ • • Date:__________

Trail Notes: _______________________________________________

_______________________________________________

_______________________________________________

_______________________________________________

☐ • • Date:__________

Trail Notes: _______________________________________________

_______________________________________________

_______________________________________________

_______________________________________________

☐ • • Date:__________

Trail Notes: _______________________________________________

_______________________________________________

_______________________________________________

_______________________________________________

## 📍 Trailward Finds

☐ DATE:

☐ DATE:

☐ DATE:

☐ DATE:

☐ DATE:

# Blanco State Park

☐ **PUMPHOUSE TRAIL**     0.3 mi. • (round trip)     Easy                    Date:__________

Designed for all ages, this level interpretive path offers a gentle walk with views over the Blanco River. Along the way, listen and look for birds overhead and turtles along the water's edge.

Trail Notes: _________________________________________________________

_____________________________________________________________________

_____________________________________________________________________


☐ **CASWELL NATURE TRAIL**     0.8 mi. • (round trip)     Easy                    Date:__________

This rocky hike passes through riverside woodland and offers a distinctive look at a dam built by the Civilian Conservation Corps during the 1930s.

Trail Notes: _________________________________________________________

_____________________________________________________________________

_____________________________________________________________________


## 📍 Trailward Finds

☐ **THE FALLS**
DATE:

☐ **CCC DAM**
DATE:

☐ **CASWELL NATURE TRAIL**
DATE:

☐ **CCC PICNIC PAVILION**
DATE:

☐ **SCENIC VIEW**
DATE:

Park Website          Trail Map

Visit the Texas Parks & Wildlife
Department at tpwd.texas.gov

# Colorado Bend State Park

☐ **SPICEWOOD SPRINGS TRAIL** — 1.3 mi. • Moderate/Difficult • 1.5 hrs. Date:_________

Clear pools and cascading waterfalls shape the landscape along this route, all fed by Spicewood Springs. The path crosses the creek multiple times before climbing the canyon, rewarding careful footing with sweeping views above.

Trail Notes: _______________________________________________________

___________________________________________________________________

___________________________________________________________________

☐ **SPICEWOOD CANYON TRAIL** — 3.0 mi. • Moderate • 2.5 hrs. Date:_________

Running along a high ridgeline, this route offers sweeping views down to the pools and waterfalls of Spicewood Springs Creek, along with long vistas across the Colorado River canyon.

Trail Notes: _______________________________________________________

___________________________________________________________________

___________________________________________________________________

☐ **RIVER TRAIL** — 3.4 mi. • Easy • 2 hrs. Date:_________

A thick overhead canopy shades this easy-to-follow route, which also provides convenient access to the river.

Trail Notes: _______________________________________________________

___________________________________________________________________

___________________________________________________________________

☐ **LEMONS RIDGE PASS** — 5.0 mi. • Moderate • 3 hrs. Date:_________

Starting near the River Backpack Camping Area, this route climbs out of the canyon and ascends westward along Lemons Ridge, ending in the uplands near the Windmill Area.

Trail Notes: _______________________________________________________

___________________________________________________________________

___________________________________________________________________

☐ **CEDAR CHOPPER LOOP** — 2.3 mi. • Moderate • 1.5 hrs. Date:_________

Mostly level ground carries this loop through cedar brakes, with scattered rocky stretches adding variety along the way.

Trail Notes: _______________________________________________________

___________________________________________________________________

___________________________________________________________________

*Continued on next page*   

# Colorado Bend State Park

☐ **GORMAN SPRING TRAIL**   0.5 mi. • Easy • 30 min   Date:________

Dense plant growth lines this route as it winds through Gorman Canyon, where multiple creek crossings require careful footing.

Trail Notes: ___________________________________

_______________________________________________

_______________________________________________

☐ **GORMAN FALLS TRAIL**   1.5 mi. • Difficult • 1.5 hrs.   Date:________
(one way)

Expect exposed terrain and heavy rock underfoot on this well-traveled route, with minimal shade and a slick, steep drop near the waterfall. Extra water is essential, and hikers should pace themselves according to their ability.

Trail Notes: ___________________________________

_______________________________________________

_______________________________________________

☐ **LIVELY LOOP**   4.8 mi • Easy • 3 hrs.   Date:________

Rolling hill country views open up along this stretch.

Trail Notes: ___________________________________

_______________________________________________

_______________________________________________

☐ **WINDMILL TRAIL**   1.6 mi. • Moderate • 1.5 hrs.   Date:________

Native grasses and seasonal wildflowers cover the rolling upland prairie along this route, which ends at a historic windmill once used to supply water for cattle.

Trail Notes: ___________________________________

_______________________________________________

_______________________________________________

☐ **DRY CREEK JUNCTION**   0.3 mi. • Easy • 15 min.   Date:________

This route crosses open prairie grasslands, punctuated by occasional rocky outcrops.

Trail Notes: ___________________________________

_______________________________________________

_______________________________________________

# Colorado Bend State Park

☐ **DOGLEG CANYON TRAIL**   1.3 mi.  •  Difficult  •  1.5 hrs.   Date:_________

Cliff faces and the canyon rim come into view along this route, revealing one of the park's quieter scenic highlights.

Trail Notes: _______________________________________________

_______________________________________________

_______________________________________________

☐ **OLD GORMAN ROAD TRAIL**   1.0 mi.  •  Moderate  •  30 min.   Date:_________

Panoramic vistas unfold along this former pasture road, now serving as a scenic hiking route.

Trail Notes: _______________________________________________

_______________________________________________

_______________________________________________

☐ **TIE SLIDE TRAIL**   2.3 mi.  •  Moderate  •  1.5 hrs.   Date:_________

Unusual rock formations line this hike, leading to the Tie Slide Overlook, where expansive views stretch across the Colorado River.

Trail Notes: _______________________________________________

_______________________________________________

_______________________________________________

☐ **TINAJA TRAIL**   2.8 mi.  •  Difficult  •  2.5 hrs.   Date:_________

This route delivers the park's toughest challenge, climbing and descending through a canyon via tight switchbacks before opening up to sweeping, high-elevation views.

Trail Notes: _______________________________________________

_______________________________________________

_______________________________________________

*Continued on next page*   

# Colorado Bend State Park

GORMAN-WINDMILL CONNECTION    0.5 mi.       Date:________

Trail Notes: _______________________________________

_______________________________________

_______________________________________

## Trailward Finds

- [ ] **SPICEWOOD SPRINGS CREEK**
  DATE:

- [ ] **GORMAN CAVE**
  DATE:

- [ ] **DOGLEG CANYON**
  DATE:

- [ ] **TINAJA**
  DATE:

- [ ] **GORMAN SPRING**
  DATE:

- [ ] **GORMAN FALLS**
  DATE:

- [ ] **TIE SLIDE OVERLOOK**
  DATE:

Park Website      Trail Map

Visit the Texas Parks & Wildlife
Department at tpwd.texas.gov

# Enchanted Rock State Natural Area

☐ INTERPRETIVE LOOP  0.5 mi. • Easy – Moderate • 25 min.  Date:_________

Near the base of Little Rock, this short path offers a close-up look at plants and wildlife adapted to the area. The trail remains open after sunset.

Trail Notes: _______________________________________________

_______________________________________________

_______________________________________________

☐ LOOP TRAIL  4.6 mi. • Moderate – Difficult • 2.5 hrs.  Date:_________

Circling the park's outer edge, this granite-lined route offers expansive views across the natural landscape. Be sure to carry ample water, and bring a flashlight if you plan to stay for stargazing. The trail remains open after dark.

Trail Notes: _______________________________________________

_______________________________________________

_______________________________________________

☐ TURKEY PASS TRAIL  0.7 mi. • Moderate • 45 min.  Date:_________

Sweeping views unfold on both sides of this route, with Enchanted Rock rising in one direction and Turkey Peak and Freshman Mountain visible on the other.

Trail Notes: _______________________________________________

_______________________________________________

_______________________________________________

☐ BASE TRAIL  0.9 mi. • Moderate • 30 min.  Date:_________

Accessed from either the Turkey Pass Trail or the Echo Canyon Trail, this route wraps around the back side of Enchanted Rock, offering a fresh perspective away from the main views.

Trail Notes: _______________________________________________

_______________________________________________

_______________________________________________

☐ ECHO CANYON TRAIL  0.7 mi. • Moderate – Challenging • 45 min.  Date:_________

This route wraps around Moss Lake before rising into the gap between Little Rock and Enchanted Rock, where massive granite boulders provide shaded places to pause.

Trail Notes: _______________________________________________

_______________________________________________

_______________________________________________

# Enchanted Rock State Natural Area

☐ SUMMIT TRAIL    0.8 mi. • Challenging • 45 min.    Date:__________

This route climbs to the summit of Enchanted Rock, where rare vernal pools sometimes form. These fragile habitats support fairy shrimp and rock quillwort, so please avoid disturbing them.

Trail Notes: __________________________________________

________________________________________________________

________________________________________________________

☐ SCENIC VIEW TRAIL    0.1 mi. • Moderate • 10 min.    Date:__________

Starting from the south end of the Loop Trail, this brief hike leads to scenic views across the surrounding Texas Hill Country. The trail remains open after sunset.

Trail Notes: __________________________________________

________________________________________________________

________________________________________________________

☐ FRONTSIDE TRAIL    0.3 mi. • Moderate • 20 min.    Date:__________

Beginning at the base of Enchanted Rock, this shaded oak-lined route provides a connection to the Turkey Pass Trail.

Trail Notes: __________________________________________

________________________________________________________

________________________________________________________

☐ BUZZARD'S ROOST TRAIL    0.7 mi.    Date:__________

Trail Notes: __________________________________________

________________________________________________________

________________________________________________________

☐ CONNECTING TRAIL    0.2 mi.    Date:__________

Trail Notes: __________________________________________

________________________________________________________

________________________________________________________

☐ MOSS LAKE TRAIL    0.6 mi.    Date:__________

Trail Notes: __________________________________________

________________________________________________________

________________________________________________________

# Enchanted Rock State Natural Area

CONNECTING TRAIL — 0.4 mi. — Date:_________

Trail Notes: _________________________________________

_____________________________________________________

_____________________________________________________

WALNUT SPRINGS TRAIL — 0.8 mi. — Date:_________

Trail Notes: _________________________________________

_____________________________________________________

_____________________________________________________

## Trailward Finds

INTERPRETIVE LOOP
DATE:

LITTLE ROCK
DATE:

ENCHANTED ROCK SUMMIT
DATE:

BUZZARD'S ROOST
DATE:

MOSS LAKE
DATE:

ECHO CANYON
DATE:

SCENIC OVERLOOK
DATE:

Park Website    Trail Map
Visit the Texas Parks & Wildlife
Department at tpwd.texas.gov

# Garner State Park

☐ OLD ENTRANCE ROAD   0.8 mi.  •   Easy   •  20 min.   Date:___________

This paved route allows both hiking and biking and is especially popular in spring, when golden-cheeked warblers may be spotted. A steep grade adds a challenging stretch along the way.

Trail Notes: ________________________________________________

___________________________________________________________

___________________________________________________________

☐ DONOVAN TRAIL   0.7 mi. •  Moderate •  30 min.   Date:___________

This route offers a close look at several of the Hill Country's most characteristic habitats.

Trail Notes: ________________________________________________

___________________________________________________________

___________________________________________________________

☐ BRIDGES TRAIL   0.7 mi. •  Challenging •  45 min.   Date:___________

Loose rock and steep sections call for careful footing along this climb. The payoff comes at Painted Rock Overlook, where views stretch toward Old Baldy and a massive Ashe juniper offers welcome shade.

Trail Notes: ________________________________________________

___________________________________________________________

___________________________________________________________

☐ CRYSTAL CAVE TRAIL   0.6 mi. •  Challenging •  45 min.   Date:___________

Several demanding sections lead hikers to one of the park's standout natural features.

Trail Notes: ________________________________________________

___________________________________________________________

___________________________________________________________

☐ BLINN RIVER TRAIL   0.5 mi. •  Moderate •  20 min.   Date:___________

A gentle walk follows the banks of the Frio River, where wildlife is often active along the water's edge. Because erosion can close this route, it's best to check with park staff before heading out.

Trail Notes: ________________________________________________

___________________________________________________________

___________________________________________________________

# Garner State Park

<table>
<tr><td>☐</td><td>OLD BALDY TRAIL</td><td>0.5 mi. • Challenging • 45 min.</td><td>Date:__________</td></tr>
</table>

A brief but demanding climb leads to an elevated overlook above the Frio River canyon. Steep, rocky footing makes careful steps essential.

Trail Notes: _______________________________________________

_______________________________________________

_______________________________________________

<table>
<tr><td>☐</td><td>FOSHEE TRAIL</td><td>1.7 mi. • Moderate • 1 hr.</td><td>Date:__________</td></tr>
</table>

Serving as a central corridor, the Foshee Trail connects with numerous routes and provides access to much of the backcountry across the rugged hills of Garner State Park.

Trail Notes: _______________________________________________

_______________________________________________

_______________________________________________

<table>
<tr><td>☐</td><td>ASHE JUNIPER TRAIL</td><td>2.5 mi. • Moderate • 1.5 hrs.</td><td>Date:__________</td></tr>
</table>

Views of the lesser-seen backside of Old Baldy open up along this route.

Trail Notes: _______________________________________________

_______________________________________________

_______________________________________________

<table>
<tr><td>☐</td><td>OLD HORSE TRAIL</td><td>0.5 mi. • Moderate • 30 min.</td><td>Date:__________</td></tr>
</table>

This narrow, historic horse path cuts across a steep mountainside, winding through the trees high above the Old Entrance Road.

Trail Notes: _______________________________________________

_______________________________________________

_______________________________________________

<table>
<tr><td>☐</td><td>FRIO CANYON TRAIL</td><td>2.9 mi. • Easy • 1.5 hrs.</td><td>Date:__________</td></tr>
</table>

This mostly level route is open to hikers and cyclists and offers sweeping views across the expanse of the Frio Canyon, with surrounding mountains visible in every direction.

Trail Notes: _______________________________________________

_______________________________________________

_______________________________________________

*Continued on next page* 

# Garner State Park

☐ NATURE TRAIL      0.6 mi.      Date:__________

Trail Notes: ______________________________________

______________________________________

______________________________________

☐ MADRONE WALKWAY    0.7 mi.      Date:__________
(hiking/biking)

Trail Notes: ______________________________________

______________________________________

______________________________________

☐ WHITE ROCK CAVE TRAIL      0.3 mi.      Date:__________

Trail Notes: ______________________________________

______________________________________

______________________________________

☐ WILD HORSE CREEK TRAIL      0.5 mi.      Date:__________

Trail Notes: ______________________________________

______________________________________

______________________________________

☐ HIGHWAY TRAIL      0.6 mi.      Date:__________
(hiking/biking)

Trail Notes: ______________________________________

______________________________________

______________________________________

☐ CAMPOS TRAIL      0.7 mi.      Date:__________

Trail Notes: ______________________________________

______________________________________

______________________________________

☐ WILKS TRAIL      1.0 mi.      Date:__________

Trail Notes: ______________________________________

______________________________________

______________________________________

# Garner State Park

☐ OLD CCC TRAIL          0.5 mi.                    Date:_________

Trail Notes: ________________________________________________

____________________________________________________________

____________________________________________________________


☐ POLLY TRAIL            0.09 mi.                   Date:_________

Trail Notes: ________________________________________________

____________________________________________________________

____________________________________________________________


☐ BELL TRAIL             0.09 mi.                   Date:_________

Trail Notes: ________________________________________________

____________________________________________________________

____________________________________________________________


☐ RIM TRAIL              0.22 mi.                   Date:_________

Trail Notes: ________________________________________________

____________________________________________________________

____________________________________________________________


☐ BIRD TRAIL             0.15 mi.                   Date:_________

Trail Notes: ________________________________________________

____________________________________________________________

____________________________________________________________


☐ CONNECTOR TRAIL        0.06 mi.                   Date:_________

Trail Notes: ________________________________________________

____________________________________________________________

____________________________________________________________

*Continued on next page*   

# Garner State Park

## 📍 Trailward Finds

- ☐ **OLD ENTRANCE ROAD OVERLOOK**
  DATE:

- ☐ **SHADY OAK**
  DATE:

- ☐ **CRYSTAL CAVE**
  DATE:

- ☐ **PAINTED ROCK OVERLOOK**
  DATE:

- ☐ **OLD ROCK FENCE**
  DATE:

- ☐ **OLD BALDY SUMMIT**
  DATE:

- ☐ **CCC HORSESHOE FOOTPRINT BOLLARDS**
  DATE:

- ☐ **CAMPOS TRAIL OVERLOOK**
  DATE:

- ☐ **OLD CCC ENTRANCE**
  DATE:

Park Website    Trail Map

Visit the Texas Parks & Wildlife
Department at tpwd.texas.gov

# Guadalupe River State Park

☐ OAK SAVANNAH LOOP  0.5 mi.  •  Easy  •  30 min.  Date:________

This brief walk passes through a restored oak savanna, offering a glimpse of a landscape that once stretched across much of this region of Texas.

Trail Notes: ________________________________________

________________________________________

________________________________________

☐ PAINTED BUNTING TRAIL  3.1 mi.  •  Moderate  •  1.5 hrs.  Date:________

Taking its name from a familiar summer songbird, this route stretches farther than any other trail in the park.

Trail Notes: ________________________________________

________________________________________

________________________________________

☐ RIVER OVERLOOK TRAIL  0.3 mi.  •  Moderate  •  45 min.  Date:________

This mostly level route ends at a riverside cliff, opening up scenic views across the valley toward the Bauer Unit.

Trail Notes: ________________________________________

________________________________________

________________________________________

☐ CEDAR SAGE RIVER TRAIL  0.4 mi.  •  Easy  •  15 min.  Date:________

This route leads hikers to two highlights—the Discovery Center and the scenic Guadalupe River.

Trail Notes: ________________________________________

________________________________________

________________________________________

☐ DISCOVERY CENTER LOOP  0.3 mi.  •  Easy  •  25 min.  Date:________

This gentle loop offers a simple woodland stroll that's well suited for families with young children.

Trail Notes: ________________________________________

________________________________________

________________________________________

*Continued on next page*   

# Guadalupe River State Park

☐ BALD CYPRESS TRAIL   0.6 mi.  •   Easy   •  30 min.   Date:__________

This route opens up extended access to the Guadalupe River within the park.

Trail Notes: ________________________________________________

________________________________________________

________________________________________________

☐ BAMBERGER TRAIL   1.7 mi.  •  Moderate to Challenging  •  2 hrs.   Date:__________

A downhill stretch from the parking area passes through classic Hill Country forest. During spring—especially mid-March through May—listen for the distinctive song of the golden-cheeked warbler.

Trail Notes: ________________________________________________

________________________________________________

________________________________________________

☐ HOFHEINZ TRAIL   1.5 mi.  •  Moderate  •  45 min.   Date:__________

This route moves from an Ashe juniper thicket into a rocky mixed hardwood forest before opening onto a bright, sunlit field.

Trail Notes: ________________________________________________

________________________________________________

________________________________________________

☐ GOLDENCHEEKED WARBLER TRAIL   0.9 mi.  •  Moderate to Challenging  •  1 hr.   Date:__________

A steep descent drops into a striking stand of old-growth oaks, with the reminder that the climb back out is just as demanding.

Trail Notes: ________________________________________________

________________________________________________

________________________________________________

☐ LITTLE BLUESTEM LOOP   0.7 mi.  •   Easy   •  30 min.   Date:__________

Once used for farming, this floodplain loop now circles an important remnant of native prairie grasses, including the species that gives the trail its name.

Trail Notes: ________________________________________________

________________________________________________

________________________________________________

# Guadalupe River State Park

☐ **CURRY CREEK OVERLOOK TRAIL**    1.2 mi. • Moderate to Challenging • 1 hr.    Date:_________

A shaded hillside route runs above Curry Creek, welcoming both hikers and cyclists. Along the way, changing terrain reveals spring-fed seeps and distinctive karst formations.

Trail Notes: _______________________________________

_______________________________________

_______________________________________

☐ **RIVER ACCESS TRAIL**    0.2 mi. • Easy • 15 min.    Date:_________

This route requires a careful river crossing—be prepared to wade by removing shoes and rolling up pant legs.

Trail Notes: _______________________________________

_______________________________________

_______________________________________

☐ **PRAIRIE TRAIL**    0.4 mi.    Date:_________

Trail Notes: _______________________________________

_______________________________________

_______________________________________

☐ **PERSIMMON PATH**    0.3 mi.    Date:_________

Trail Notes: _______________________________________

_______________________________________

_______________________________________

☐ **LIVE OAK TRAIL**    0.8 mi.    Date:_________

Trail Notes: _______________________________________

_______________________________________

_______________________________________

☐ **BARRED OWL TRAIL**    0.8 mi.    Date:_________

Trail Notes: _______________________________________

_______________________________________

_______________________________________

*Continued on next page*    

# Guadalupe River State Park

☐ TURKEY SINK TRAIL   0.2 mi.       Date:_________

Trail Notes: ______________________________________________________

__________________________________________________________________

__________________________________________________________________

☐ BAUER TRAIL   1.3 mi.       Date:_________

Trail Notes: ______________________________________________________

__________________________________________________________________

__________________________________________________________________

☐ HOFHEINZ CONNECTOR   0.2 mi.       Date:_________

Trail Notes: ______________________________________________________

__________________________________________________________________

__________________________________________________________________

## 📍 Trailward Finds

☐ RUST HOUSE
DATE:

☐ DISCOVERY CENTER
DATE:

☐ SCENIC OVERLOOK
DATE:

☐ GUADALUPE RIVER RAPIDS
DATE:

☐ SWALLOW CLIFF
DATE:

☐ BAUER UNIT
DATE:

**Park Website**     **Trail Map**

Visit the Texas Parks & Wildlife
Department at tpwd.texas.gov

# Inks Lake State Park

**BLUEBONNET TRAIL**  0.6 mi. • Moderate • 30 min.  Date:_________

Rocky outcrops and rolling terrain define this route, where a wide mix of cactus and tree species can be seen along the way.

Trail Notes: _________________________________________________

_________________________________________________

_________________________________________________

**DEVIL'S WATERHOLE NATURE TRAIL**  0.2 mi. • Easy • 7 min.  Date:_________

This short connector links the parking lot with Devil's Waterhole and the Valley Spring Creek Trail. After an initial steep climb, the path levels out and is suitable for strollers and some wheelchairs.

Trail Notes: _________________________________________________

_________________________________________________

_________________________________________________

**LAKE TRAIL**  1.2 mi. • Easy to Moderate • 45 min.  Date:_________

This trail follows Stumpy Hollow through wooded lowlands to rocky outcrops and seasonal vernal pools—fragile habitat for species like fairy shrimp and rock quillwort. Access is from park headquarters or the Angler's Trails.

Trail Notes: _________________________________________________

_________________________________________________

_________________________________________________

**PECAN FLATS TRAIL**  1.8 mi. • Moderate • 1.5 hrs.  Date:_________

This trail begins with a wide, level walk through a pecan forest suitable for strollers and some wheelchairs, then turns rugged beyond the Cutoff Trail with scenic views and seasonal wildflowers. Parking is available near park headquarters or along Park Road 4 (no overnight parking).

Trail Notes: _________________________________________________

_________________________________________________

_________________________________________________

**VALLEY SPRING CREEK TRAIL**  0.9 mi. • Easy • 45 min.  Date:_________

Beginning at Devil's Waterhole, this route follows Spring Creek before looping back through oak, juniper, and mesquite woodland.

Trail Notes: _________________________________________________

_________________________________________________

_________________________________________________

# Inks Lake State Park

☐ **WOODLAND TRAIL**      2.2 mi. • Moderate • 1.5 hrs.      Date:__________

This rugged, mostly unshaded backcountry route crosses oak woodland and rocky outcrops with scenic views—bring plenty of water. Access from Park Road 4 or connect via the Lake Trail and Woodland Trail.

Trail Notes: __________________________________________

________________________________________________________

________________________________________________________

☐ **DEVIL'S BACKBONE NATURE TRAIL**      1.3 mi. • Moderate • 1 hr.      Date:__________

This interpretive trail features views of Inks Lake and lakeshore geology. Access is from the Valley Spring Creek Trail or the Bird Blind off Park Road 4 (gate code at HQ).

Trail Notes: __________________________________________

________________________________________________________

________________________________________________________

☐ **ANGLER'S TRAILS**      1.0 mi. •      Easy      • 30 min.      Date:__________

Narrow singletrack routes branch from the South Fishing Pier and nearby camping loops, leading down to the lake and several productive fishing areas. Contains Upper and Lower Angler's Trails.

Trail Notes: __________________________________________

________________________________________________________

________________________________________________________

☐ **UPPER ANGLER'S TRAIL**      0.5 mi.      Date:__________

Trail Notes: __________________________________________

________________________________________________________

________________________________________________________

☐ **LOWER ANGLER'S TRAIL**      0.5 mi.      Date:__________

Trail Notes: __________________________________________

________________________________________________________

________________________________________________________

☐ **AMPHITHEATER TRAIL**      0.1 mi.      Date:__________

Trail Notes: __________________________________________

________________________________________________________

________________________________________________________

# Inks Lake State Park

☐ CUTOFF TRAIL          0.13 mi.                    Date:__________

Trail Notes: ____________________________________________

____________________________________________

____________________________________________

## 📍 Trailward Finds

☐ **BIRD BLIND**
DATE:

☐ **VALLEY SPRING CREEK WATERFALL**
DATE:

☐ **DEVIL'S WATERHOLE SCENIC OVERLOOK**
DATE:

☐ **DEVIL'S WATERHOLE**
DATE:

☐ **SPRING CREEK DELTA**
DATE:

☐ **PARK ROAD 4**
DATE:

☐ **STUMPY HOLLOW**
DATE:

☐ **1000 FT OVERLOOK OF INKS LAKE**
DATE:

Park Website          Trail Map
Visit the Texas Parks & Wildlife
Department at tpwd.texas.gov

# Lake Brownwood State Park

☐ TEXAS OAK TRAIL    1.4 mi. • Moderate • 45 min.    Date:_________

This trail showcases several Texas oak species, including Texas red, post, and live oaks.

Trail Notes: ___________________________________________________

_______________________________________________________________

_______________________________________________________________


☐ OPOSSUM LOOP    0.3 mi. •    Easy    • 30 min.    Date:_________

Wildlife is often spotted along this route or from the viewing blind, including opossums, white-tailed deer, and wild turkeys.

Trail Notes: ___________________________________________________

_______________________________________________________________

_______________________________________________________________


☐ COUNCIL BLUFF TRAIL    0.3 mi. • Moderate • 30 min.    Date:_________

Stone steps lead to bluff-top views overlooking the lake.

Trail Notes: ___________________________________________________

_______________________________________________________________

_______________________________________________________________


☐ LAKESIDE TRAIL    0.7 mi. • Moderate • 45 min.    Date:_________

This historic route links the campground and cabins with the day-use area, showcasing work by the Civilian Conservation Corps. Limestone tables and benches along the way offer scenic views of Lake Brownwood.

Trail Notes: ___________________________________________________

_______________________________________________________________

_______________________________________________________________


☐ PUMP HOUSE TRAIL    0.02 mi. • Moderate • 10 min.    Date:_________

This short spur leads to the park's original stone pump house, built by the Civilian Conservation Corps to supply water.

Trail Notes: ___________________________________________________

_______________________________________________________________

_______________________________________________________________

# Lake Brownwood State Park

☐ **NOPALES RIDGE TRAIL**   2.8 mi. • Moderate • 2.5 hrs.   Date:_________

Prickly pear cacti line this route, so watch for sharp spines while hiking or biking. Twisted-leaf yucca—whose name means "lover of rock"—also grows here.

Trail Notes: _______________________________________________

_______________________________________________

_______________________________________________

☐ **OFFICE TRAIL**   0.2 mi.   Date:_________

Trail Notes: _______________________________________________

_______________________________________________

_______________________________________________

## ⚲ Trailward Finds

☐ **CCC GRAND STAIRWAY**
DATE:

☐ **CCC PICNIC SITE**
DATE:

☐ **CCC WATER PUMPHOUSE**
DATE:

☐ **CCC AND 36TH DIVISION MEMORIAL MONUMENTS**
DATE:

☐ **COUNCIL BLUFF PAVILION AND OVERLOOK**
DATE:

☐ **TEXAS OAK TRAIL OVERLOOK**
DATE:

☐ **LIMESTONE BOULDERS**
DATE:

Park Website     Trail Map

Visit the Texas Parks & Wildlife
Department at tpwd.texas.gov

# Lake Somerville State Park
## Nails Creek Unit

☐ **LAKE SOMERVILLE TRAILWAY**     13.4 mi. • Challenging • 6+ hrs.     Date:________

The Lake Somerville Trailway offers miles of outdoor access for hikers, cyclists, anglers, equestrians, and backpackers. Begin at the Birch Creek Unit or Nails Creek Unit, or enter mid-trail from the Newman Bottom. Check with park headquarters for current trail conditions before heading out.

Trail Notes: __________________________________________________

_____________________________________________________________

_____________________________________________________________


☐ **CEDAR CREEK LOOP**     2.1 mi. • Moderate • 1.5 hrs.     Date:________

As the longest loop at the Nails Creek Unit, this quiet route is well suited for fishing access and wildlife watching.

Trail Notes: __________________________________________________

_____________________________________________________________

_____________________________________________________________


☐ **NAILS CREEK LOOP**     0.8 mi. •     Easy     • 30 min.     Date:________

This brief route blends wooded shade with open stretches that reveal sweeping lake views.

Trail Notes: __________________________________________________

_____________________________________________________________

_____________________________________________________________


☐ **OVERLOOK TRAIL**     0.7 mi. •     Easy     • 30 min.     Date:________

This short hike leads to a scenic overlook, with options to extend your outing by connecting to the Rocky Point Trail or the Whitetail Run Trail.

Trail Notes: __________________________________________________

_____________________________________________________________

_____________________________________________________________

# Lake Somerville State Park

## Nails Creek Unit

☐ LAKE SHORE TRAIL    0.7 mi. •    Easy    • 20 min.    Date:__________

This flat lakeside path is rich with birds, butterflies, and insects among the tall grasses—sun protection recommended.

Trail Notes: ________________________________________________

____________________________________________________________

____________________________________________________________

☐ COLVIN HILL BYPASS    0.6 mi.    Date:__________

Trail Notes: ________________________________________________

____________________________________________________________

____________________________________________________________

☐ WHITETAIL RUN TRAIL    0.7 mi.    Date:__________

Trail Notes: ________________________________________________

____________________________________________________________

____________________________________________________________

☐ ROCKY POINT TRAIL    0.2 mi.    Date:__________

Trail Notes: ________________________________________________

____________________________________________________________

____________________________________________________________

☐ COYOTE CROSSING    0.1 mi.    Date:__________

Trail Notes: ________________________________________________

____________________________________________________________

____________________________________________________________

☐ BENT TREE TRAIL    0.4 mi.    Date:__________

Trail Notes: ________________________________________________

____________________________________________________________

____________________________________________________________

*Continued on next page*    

# Lake Somerville State Park

## Nails Creek Unit

☐ **NAILS CREEK ACCESS ROAD**  0.4 mi.  Date:__________

Trail Notes: _______________________________

_______________________________

_______________________________

☐ **CHANNEL LOOP**  1.4 mi.  Date:__________

Trail Notes: _______________________________

_______________________________

_______________________________

## 📍 Trailward Finds

☐ **SCENIC VIEWPOINT**
DATE:

☐ **PICNIC HILL**
DATE:

☐ **ROCKY POINT**
DATE:

☐ **OVERLOOK PLATFORM**
DATE:

☐ **TRAILWAY TRAILHEAD**
DATE:

Park Website    Trail Map

Visit the Texas Parks & Wildlife
Department at tpwd.texas.gov

# Lake Somerville State Park

## Birch Creek Unit

☐ **LAKE SOMERVILLE TRAILWAY**  13.4 mi. • Challenging • 6+ hrs.  Date:__________

The Lake Somerville Trailway offers miles of outdoor access for hikers, cyclists, anglers, equestrians, and backpackers. Begin at the Birch Creek Unit or Nails Creek Unit, or enter mid-trail from the Newman Bottom. Check with park headquarters for current trail conditions before heading out.

Trail Notes: _______________________________________________

_________________________________________________________

_________________________________________________________

☐ **WILDERNESS RUN**  1.3 mi. • Moderate • 1 hr.  Date:__________

This peaceful route winds through the park with opportunities for wildlife sightings and connections to the Sunset Trail and Bucktail Run Trail for a longer hike.

Trail Notes: _______________________________________________

_________________________________________________________

_________________________________________________________

☐ **BLUESTEM BEND TRAIL**  1.0 mi. • Easy • 30 min.  Date:__________

This easy lakeside route traces the shoreline to a scenic confluence where Birch Creek meets Somerville Lake—sun protection recommended.

Trail Notes: _______________________________________________

_________________________________________________________

_________________________________________________________

☐ **EAGLE POINT TRAIL**  0.4 mi. • Easy • 20 min.  Date:__________

This short hike leads to a scenic overlook and a shaded oak—an ideal picnic spot and a good place to watch for nesting bald eagles.

Trail Notes: _______________________________________________

_________________________________________________________

_________________________________________________________

☐ **BEAUTYBERRY TRAIL**  0.9 mi. • Moderate • 1 hr.  Date:__________

Wildflowers line this quiet path, attracting pollinators throughout the seasons—bring a camera to capture the changing colors.

Trail Notes: _______________________________________________

_________________________________________________________

_________________________________________________________

*Continued on next page*  

# Lake Somerville State Park

## Birch Creek Unit

☐ **BUCKTAIL RUN**     0.7 mi. •     Easy     • 45 min.     Date:_________

This wooded connector links the Wilderness Run Trail and the Beautyberry Trail, passing near the Family Fishing Pond—bring a pole to try fishing.

Trail Notes: _______________________________________________

_______________________________________________

_______________________________________________

☐ **HONEYBEE HILL TRAIL**     0.4 mi. •     Easy     • 20 min.     Date:_________

This hard-packed, accessible loop offers shaded walking and birdsong, you can extend your hike by connecting to the Lake Somerville Trailway.

Trail Notes: _______________________________________________

_______________________________________________

_______________________________________________

☐ **SUNSET TRAIL**     0.9 mi. • Moderate •   1 hr.     Date:_________

As evening approaches, this path winds through mature hardwoods and native grasses, with lake waves in the distance and owls beginning to call.

Trail Notes: _______________________________________________

_______________________________________________

_______________________________________________

☐ **CARDINAL BEND**     0.6 mi. •     Easy     • 30 min.     Date:_________

This easy loop is great for spotting wildlife like northern cardinals, with connections to the Wilderness Run Trail and the Bucktail Run Trail.

Trail Notes: _______________________________________________

_______________________________________________

_______________________________________________

☐ **CEDAR LOOP**     0.1 mi.     Date:_________

Trail Notes: _______________________________________________

_______________________________________________

_______________________________________________

☐ **HQ LAKE TRAIL**     0.1 mi.     Date:_________

Trail Notes: _______________________________________________

_______________________________________________

_______________________________________________

# Lake Somerville State Park
## Birch Creek Unit

☐ PINTAIL TRAIL          0.8 mi.                    Date:___________

Trail Notes: _______________________________________________

______________________________________________________________

______________________________________________________________

## 📍 Trailward Finds

☐ BIRCH CREEK FISHING JETTY
DATE:

☐ CISTERN
DATE:

☐ EAGLE POINT
DATE:

☐ TRAILWAY ENTRANCE
DATE:

Park Website        Trail Map

Visit the Texas Parks & Wildlife
Department at tpwd.texas.gov

# Lake Somerville State Park

## Complex (Trailway)

☐ **FLAG POND LOOP** — 1.7 mi. • Easy • 1 hr. — Date:_________

Open sightlines along this trail provide clear views of Flag Pond, along with the water-control features used as a habitat for migratory birds.

Trail Notes: _______________________________________________

_______________________________________________

_______________________________________________

☐ **ALLIGATOR LOOP** — 1.5 mi. • Moderate • 1.25 hrs. — Date:_________

A sandy descent leads to this loop along Yegua Creek, a good spot for fishing and occasional alligator sightings along the bank.

Trail Notes: _______________________________________________

_______________________________________________

_______________________________________________

☐ **GERDES SPUR** — 1.6 mi. • Moderate • 1.5 hrs. — Date:_________

Once a ranch road, this spur now offers equestrians a quiet, secluded ride.

Trail Notes: _______________________________________________

_______________________________________________

_______________________________________________

☐ **SANDY SLOUGH TRAIL** — 2.1 mi. • Moderate • 2 hrs. — Date:_________

Often considered one of the most scenic routes in the Lake Somerville State Park Complex, this primitive trail follows Yegua Creek through mature hardwoods and seasonal wetlands. Check with headquarters for current conditions.

Trail Notes: _______________________________________________

_______________________________________________

_______________________________________________

☐ **MESA SPUR TRAIL** — 0.5 mi. — Date:_________

Trail Notes: _______________________________________________

_______________________________________________

☐ **MESA SPUR TRAIL** — 0.5 mi. — Date:_________

Trail Notes: _______________________________________________

_______________________________________________

# Lake Somerville State Park

## Complex (Trailway)

☐ **FLAG POND LOOP**     1.7 mi.  •  Easy  •  1 hr.     Date:___________

Open sightlines along this trail provide clear views of Flag Pond, along with the water-control features used as a habitat for migratory birds.

Trail Notes: _________________________________________________

_____________________________________________________________

_____________________________________________________________

☐ **ALLIGATOR LOOP**     1.5 mi.  •  Moderate  •  1.25 hrs.     Date:___________

A sandy descent leads to this loop along Yegua Creek, a good spot for fishing and occasional alligator sightings along the bank.

Trail Notes: _________________________________________________

_____________________________________________________________

_____________________________________________________________

☐ **GERDES SPUR**     1.6 mi.  •  Moderate  •  1.5 hrs.     Date:___________

Once a ranch road, this spur now offers equestrians a quiet, secluded ride.

Trail Notes: _________________________________________________

_____________________________________________________________

_____________________________________________________________

☐ **SANDY SLOUGH TRAIL**     2.1 mi.  •  Moderate  •  2 hrs.     Date:___________

Often considered one of the most scenic routes in the Lake Somerville State Park Complex, this primitive trail follows Yegua Creek through mature hardwoods and seasonal wetlands. Check with headquarters for current conditions.

Trail Notes: _________________________________________________

_____________________________________________________________

_____________________________________________________________

☐ **LAMB RANCH LOOP**     0.6 mi.     Date:___________

Trail Notes: _________________________________________________

_____________________________________________________________

_____________________________________________________________

*Continued on next page*     

# Lake Somerville State Park

## Complex (Trailway)

☐ WALDO'S LOOP     1.5 mi.     Date:__________

Trail Notes: ________________________________________
___________________________________________________
___________________________________________________

☐ SANDHILL TRAIL     0.4 mi.     Date:__________

Trail Notes: ________________________________________
___________________________________________________
___________________________________________________

☐ WHITE BASS RUN     1.3 mi.     Date:__________

Trail Notes: ________________________________________
___________________________________________________
___________________________________________________

☐ HORSESHOE BEND ACCESS ROAD     0.5 mi.     Date:__________

Trail Notes: ________________________________________
___________________________________________________
___________________________________________________

☐ SEHLKE THICKET TRAIL     0.6 mi.     Date:__________

Trail Notes: ________________________________________
___________________________________________________
___________________________________________________

 ## Trailward Finds

☐ NEWMAN PAD
DATE:

☐ FLAG POND
DATE:

Park Website

Trail Map

Visit the Texas Parks & Wildlife
Department at tpwd.texas.gov

# Lake Whitney State Park

☐ TWO BRIDGES TRAIL    0.9 mi.  •    Easy                    Date:__________

This loop winds through post oak forest and includes two wooden bridges crossing small creeks, adding scenic highlights for hikers and cyclists.

Trail Notes: _____________________________________________________

_____________________________________________________________

_____________________________________________________________


☐ TOWASH FOREST TRAIL    1.2 mi.  •    Easy                    Date:__________

This trail offers good birdwatching for osprey and other species, with shoreline views, traces of open prairie, and scenic looks across the lake.

Trail Notes: _____________________________________________________

_____________________________________________________________

_____________________________________________________________


## 📍 Trailward Finds

☐ BIG OAK
DATE:

☐ LAKE VIEW POINT
DATE:

☐ BASS TOURNAMENT HISTORICAL MARKER
DATE:

☐ TOWASH SETTLEMENT
DATE:

Park Website        Trail Map
Visit the Texas Parks & Wildlife
Department at tpwd.texas.gov

# Lockhart State Park

☐ CLEAR FORK TRAIL     0.4 mi. •     Easy     • 20 min.    Date:_________

This easy walk follows a riparian corridor along Clear Fork Creek, passing some of the park's largest trees and historic check dams built by the Civilian Conservation Corps.

Trail Notes: _______________________________________________

_______________________________________________

_______________________________________________

☐ WILD ROSE LOOP     0.4 mi. •     Easy     • 20 min.    Date:_________

This short loop crosses a mix of bluestem prairie, red cedar, and green ash habitats. Watch for thorns from invasive Macartney rose along the way.

Trail Notes: _______________________________________________

_______________________________________________

_______________________________________________

☐ CREEKVIEW TRAIL     0.3 mi. •     Easy     • 10 min.    Date:_________

This flat ridge walk above Clear Fork Creek leads to a good fishing spot and connects with the Fence Line Trail and Persimmon Trail.

Trail Notes: _______________________________________________

_______________________________________________

_______________________________________________

☐ HILLTOP TRAIL     0.3 mi. • Moderate • 15 min.    Date:_________

This trail climbs and descends through varied terrain, offering a changing mix of plant life to discover along the way.

Trail Notes: _______________________________________________

_______________________________________________

_______________________________________________

☐ FENCE LINE TRAIL     0.2 mi. • Moderate • 20 min.    Date:_________

This route runs along much of the park's southern edge, where the scenery shifts noticeably along the way.

Trail Notes: _______________________________________________

_______________________________________________

_______________________________________________

# Lockhart State Park

☐ PERSIMMON TRAIL    0.2 mi. • Challenging • 15 min.    Date:_________

This shaded route crosses a rugged hillside dotted with Texas persimmon trees.

Trail Notes: _______________________________________________

_______________________________________________

_______________________________________________

☐ CHISHOLM TRAIL    0.7 mi. • Moderate • 15 min.    Date:_________

Passing the third hole of the golf course, this route connects with the Rattlesnake Run, Comanche Loop, Fence Line Trail, or the CCC Trail.

Trail Notes: _______________________________________________

_______________________________________________

_______________________________________________

☐ COMANCHE LOOP    0.1 mi. •    Easy    • 10 min.    Date:_________

Named for a historic lookout used by Comanche tribes, this easy loop offers hilltop views across the park and the surrounding Lockhart area.

Trail Notes: _______________________________________________

_______________________________________________

_______________________________________________

☐ RATTLESNAKE RUN    0.5 mi. • Challenging • 20 min.    Date:_________

This is the park's most demanding route and passes near the Recreation Hall.

Trail Notes: _______________________________________________

_______________________________________________

_______________________________________________

☐ CADDY TRAIL    0.4 mi. • Moderate • 15 min.    Date:_________

Once used by golf caddies traveling between the course and clubhouse, this winding path now connects the Recreation Hall and the CCC Trail.

Trail Notes: _______________________________________________

_______________________________________________

_______________________________________________

*Continued on next page*    

# Lockhart State Park

☐ **CCC TRAIL**  0.2 mi. • Moderate • 5 min.  Date:___________

Starting behind the Recreation Hall, this trail descends historic CCC concrete steps from a hilltop view of Lockhart down to the golf course and park road.

Trail Notes: _______________________________________

_______________________________________

_______________________________________

## ⚲ Trailward Finds

☐ **CCC SWIMMING POOL**
DATE:

☐ **CCC CHECK DAM**
DATE:

☐ **HISTORIC GOLF COURSE**
DATE:

☐ **LATRINE RUINS**
DATE:

☐ **RECREATION HALL**
DATE:

☐ **WATER TOWER**
DATE:

☐ **OLD #1 TEE BOX**
DATE:

☐ **COMANCHE LOOP SCENIC VIEW**
DATE:

Park Website    Trail Map
Visit the Texas Parks & Wildlife
Department at tpwd.texas.gov

# Longhorn Cavern State Park

No official **trail map** is available for this park.

☐ **Backbone Ridge Nature Trail**    0.35 mi.    Date:_________

Trail Notes: _______________________________________

_______________________________________

_______________________________________

☐ **Karst Discovery Trail**    0.60 mi.    Date:_________

Trail Notes: _______________________________________

_______________________________________

_______________________________________

☐ **Warbler Walk**    0.08 mi.    Date:_________

Trail Notes: _______________________________________

_______________________________________

_______________________________________

☐ **Wildflower Way**    0.10 mi.    Date:_________

Trail Notes: _______________________________________

_______________________________________

_______________________________________

☐ **Comanche Spur**    0.08 mi.    Date:_________

Trail Notes: _______________________________________

_______________________________________

_______________________________________

## ◉ Trailward Finds

☐ **CCC OBSERVATION TOWER**
DATE:

☐ **CCC CABIN**
DATE:

☐ **LONGHORN CAVERN**
DATE:

☐ **VISITOR CENTER**
DATE:

Park Website    Park Map

Visit the Texas Parks & Wildlife
Department at tpwd.texas.gov

# Lost Maples State Natural Area

☐ **MAPLE TRAIL** · 0.4 mi. · Easy · 20 min. · Date:________

This brief hike passes through an impressive grove of bigtooth maples—see if you can spot the feature that inspired their name.

Trail Notes: _________________________________________________

_____________________________________________________________

_____________________________________________________________

☐ **EAST-WEST TRAIL** · 1.0 mi. · Easy · 45 min. · Date:________

This shaded route follows a tributary of the Sabinal River beneath mature trees, with options to extend your hike along the West or East trails.

Trail Notes: _________________________________________________

_____________________________________________________________

_____________________________________________________________

☐ **EAST TRAIL** · 3.1 mi. · Challenging · 3 hrs. · Date:________

This route follows the spring-fed Sabinal River past bigtooth maples and cypress before climbing rocky slopes to scenic views. Steep sections require good footing and plenty of water.

Trail Notes: _________________________________________________

_____________________________________________________________

_____________________________________________________________

☐ **WEST TRAIL** · 3.6 mi. · Challenging · 3.5 hrs. · Date:________

This steep hike leads into the shaded cool of Mystic Canyon, where springs, solitude, and scenic views reward the climb. Rocky terrain makes good footing and plenty of water essential.

Trail Notes: _________________________________________________

_____________________________________________________________

_____________________________________________________________

☐ **WEST LOOP TRAIL** · 2.9 mi. (round trip) · Moderate · 1.5 hr. · Date:________

A half-mile detour from the West Trail leads into a quiet, shaded grove of Ashe juniper.

Trail Notes: _________________________________________________

_____________________________________________________________

# Lost Maples State Natural Area

☐ **TRAIL TO DAY-USE AREA**  0.1 mi.  Date:_________

Trail Notes: _______________________________________

___________________________________________________

___________________________________________________

## 📍 Trailward Finds

☐ **MONKEY ROCK**
DATE:

☐ **GROTTO**
DATE:

☐ **SCENIC OVERLOOK**
DATE:

☐ **POND DAY-USE AREA**
DATE:

☐ **SPRING**
DATE:

☐ **SPRING**
DATE:

Park Website    Trail Map
Visit the Texas Parks & Wildlife
Department at tpwd.texas.gov

# Lyndon B. Johnson State Park

This state park emphasizes historical landmarks over hiking trails; no **Trail Map** is Available.

☐ NATURE TRAIL · · Date:_________

Trail Notes: ____________________________________________________

__________________________________________________________________

__________________________________________________________________

## 📍 Trailward Finds

Park Website  Park Map

Visit the Texas Parks & Wildlife
Department at tpwd.texas.gov

☐ RIVER OVERLOOK
DATE:

☐ INTERPRETIVE EXHIBIT
DATE:

☐ LBJ STATUE
DATE:

☐ SAUER–BECKMANN LIVING HISTORY FARM
DATE:

☐ AMERICAN BISON HERD VIEWING
DATE:

☐ OFFICIAL TEXAS LONGHORN HERD VIEWING
DATE:

☐ VISITOR CENTER COMPLEX
DATE:

☐ AQUATIC COMPLEX
DATE:

# McKinney Falls State Park

☐ ROCK SHELTER TRAIL   0.6 mi. •   Easy   • 15 min.   Date:_________

This hiking-only route offers varied scenery, including views of Onion Creek, the massive bald cypress known as Old Baldy, and the cool limestone of the Rock Shelter.

Trail Notes: _______________________________________________

_______________________________________________

_______________________________________________

☐ ONION CREEK HIKE AND BIKE TRAIL   2.8 mi. •   Easy   • 1.5 hrs.   Date:_________

This improved trail follows Onion Creek before looping through forested campground areas and is a good spot to watch for wildlife like white-tailed deer or coyotes.

Trail Notes: _______________________________________________

_______________________________________________

_______________________________________________

☐ PICNIC TRAIL   0.5 mi. •   Easy   • 15 min.   Date:_________

This short, hiking-only trail is ideal for families and leads to scenic views at the Lower Falls after a picnic break.

Trail Notes: _______________________________________________

_______________________________________________

_______________________________________________

☐ HOMESTEAD TRAIL   3.1 mi. • Moderate • 1.5 hrs.   Date:_________

This hike-and-bike trail is a great place to explore the park's history, including the McKinney Homestead, Gristmill, and Smith Family Picnic Table. Reaching the trail requires crossing the creek, so expect wet feet and use caution.

Trail Notes: _______________________________________________

_______________________________________________

_______________________________________________

☐ FLINT ROCK LOOP TRAIL   1.5 mi. • Moderate • 1 hr.   Date:_________

Rocky terrain leads into a secluded hardwood bottomland. Creek crossing required—use caution and bring water for you and your dog.

Trail Notes: _______________________________________________

_______________________________________________

_______________________________________________

*Continued on next page*   

# McKinney Falls State Park

☐ **WILLIAMSON CREEK OVERLOOK TRAIL**   1.1 mi.  •  Moderate  •  45 min.   Date:__________

Though just over a mile long, reaching this trail requires traveling sections of the Homestead and Flint Rock Loop Trails, so plan your pace. Scenic views of Williamson Creek make the effort worthwhile, and access includes a creek crossing—use caution.

Trail Notes: ________________________________________________

________________________________________________

________________________________________________

☐ **CACTUS GARDEN TRAIL**   0.5 mi.  •  Moderate  •  15 min.   Date:__________

Follow this alternate route to pass through broad stretches of prickly pear cactus. Please stay on the designated trail.

Trail Notes: ________________________________________________

________________________________________________

________________________________________________

☐ **SERVICE ROAD TRAIL**   1.1 mi.   Date:__________

Trail Notes: ________________________________________________

________________________________________________

________________________________________________

☐ **HOMESTEAD SHORTCUT TRAIL**   0.4 mi.   Date:__________

Trail Notes: ________________________________________________

________________________________________________

________________________________________________

☐ **GRISTMILL SPUR TRAIL**   0.1 mi.   Date:__________

Trail Notes: ________________________________________________

________________________________________________

________________________________________________

☐ **ARMADILLO TRAIL**   0.1 mi.   Date:__________

Trail Notes: ________________________________________________

________________________________________________

________________________________________________

# McKinney Falls State Park

## Trailward Finds

Park Website    Trail Map

Visit the Texas Parks & Wildlife
Department at tpwd.texas.gov

- ☐ HORSE TRAINER'S CABIN
  DATE:
- ☐ UPPER FALLS
  DATE:
- ☐ OLD BALDY
  DATE:
- ☐ PREHISTORIC ROCK SHELTER
  DATE:
- ☐ BOULDERING ROCKS
  DATE:
- ☐ EL CAMINO REAL
  DATE:
- ☐ LOWER FALLS
  DATE:
- ☐ MCKINNEY HOMESTEAD
  DATE:
- ☐ GRISTMILL
  DATE:
- ☐ SMITH FAMILY PICNIC AREA
  DATE:
- ☐ BLUEBONNET MEADOW
  DATE:

# Meridian State Park

☐ **BOSQUE HIKING TRAIL**    2.2 mi. • Challenging    Date:_________

This challenging trail circles Lake Meridian, offering close views of the historic CCC dam and a scenic stop at Bee Ledge overlook.

Trail Notes: _______________________________________________

___________________________________________________________

___________________________________________________________

☐ **SHINNERY RIDGE TRAIL**    1.5 mi. • Moderate    Date:_________

This easy loop is great for families, with a partially paved and accessible path. During summer, keep an eye out for golden-cheeked warblers.

Trail Notes: _______________________________________________

___________________________________________________________

___________________________________________________________

☐ **LITTLE FOREST JUNIOR TRAIL**    0.8 mi. • Easy    Date:_________

Take your time on this short, rocky trail. In spring, stop near the park road crossing to enjoy seasonal wildflowers like bluebonnets, Indian paintbrush, and firewheels.

Trail Notes: _______________________________________________

___________________________________________________________

___________________________________________________________

☐ **LITTLE SPRINGS TRAIL**    0.7 mi. • Moderate    Date:_________

Keep an eye out for wildlife along this short, rugged trail.

Trail Notes: _______________________________________________

___________________________________________________________

___________________________________________________________

☐ **WILDFLOWER TRAIL**    0.1 mi. • Easy    Date:_________

Enjoy a calm walk through colorful Texas wildflowers, with pollinators in motion and quiet lakeside views.

Trail Notes: _______________________________________________

___________________________________________________________

___________________________________________________________

# Meridian State Park

## Trailward Finds

Visit the Texas Parks & Wildlife
Department at tpwd.texas.gov

- [ ] **FERN LEDGE**
  DATE:

- [ ] **BEE LEDGE**
  DATE:

- [ ] **WILDFLOWER FIELD**
  DATE:

- [ ] **CIVILIAN CONSERVATION CORPS REFECTORY**
  DATE:

- [ ] **CIVILIAN CONSERVATION CORPS STONE GRILL**
  DATE:

- [ ] **CIVILIAN CONSERVATION CORPS BRIDGE**
  DATE:

# Mother Neff State Park

☐ PRAIRIE LOOP   0.6 mi. • Easy   Date:_________

This family-friendly walk winds through restored Washita prairie, where native grasses and wildflowers are returning. Watch for Texas songbirds and pollinators along the way.

Trail Notes: _______________________________

______________________________________________

______________________________________________

☐ POND TRAIL   0.5 mi. • Easy   Date:_________

Walk to the prairie pond and pause at the wildlife viewing blind—patient visitors may be rewarded with unexpected sightings.

Trail Notes: _______________________________

______________________________________________

______________________________________________

☐ TOWER TRAIL   0.6 mi. • Moderate   Date:_________

This trail guides hikers to a historic CCC rock tower, where a spiral stone staircase leads to scenic views. The route continues past a CCC-built picnic table and stone steps to Park Road 14—use caution in wet conditions.

Trail Notes: _______________________________

______________________________________________

______________________________________________

☐ CAVE TRAIL   0.2 mi. • Moderate   Date:_________

Follow this trail to a historic rock shelter once used by the Tonkawa more than 200 years ago.

Trail Notes: _______________________________

______________________________________________

______________________________________________

☐ WASH POND TRAIL   0.5 mi. • Moderate   Date:_________

Visit Wash Pond, a natural basin expanded by the CCC, and relax beside its clear, spring-fed waters while watching for visiting wildlife.

Trail Notes: _______________________________

______________________________________________

______________________________________________

# Mother Neff State Park

☐ BLUFF TRAIL     0.4 mi. • Moderate     Date:________

This trail follows limestone bluffs and passes through oak and Ashe juniper woodlands. Listen for the endangered golden-cheeked warbler, which relies on Ashe juniper bark for nesting.

Trail Notes: _______________________________________________

_______________________________________________

_______________________________________________

☐ PLAYGROUND TRAIL     0.2 mi.     Date:________

Trail Notes: _______________________________________________

_______________________________________________

_______________________________________________

☐ HISTORIC BELL TRAIL  0.05 mi.     Date:________

Trail Notes: _______________________________________________

_______________________________________________

_______________________________________________

## 📍 Trailward Finds

☐ **PRAIRIE POND**
DATE:

☐ **CCC ROCK TOWER**
DATE:

☐ **CCC TABLE**
DATE:

☐ **TONKAWA CAVE**
DATE:

☐ **WASH POND**
DATE:

☐ **HISTORIC BELL**
DATE:

Park Website          Trail Map

Visit the Texas Parks & Wildlife
Department at tpwd.texas.gov

# Palmetto State Park

☐ **PALMETTO INTERPRETIVE TRAIL**   0.3 mi. • Easy • 30 min.   Date:______

This short trail highlights the area's diverse habitats at the meeting point of multiple ecoregions, with interpretive panels sharing insights on local plants, wildlife, and history.

Trail Notes: _______________________________________________

_______________________________________________

_______________________________________________

☐ **OXBOW LAKE TRAIL**   0.7 mi. • Easy • 45 min.   Date:______

Enjoy an easy walk around 4-acre Oxbow Lake, a prime spot for birdwatching, including herons and kingfishers.

Trail Notes: _______________________________________________

_______________________________________________

_______________________________________________

☐ **MESQUITE FLATS TRAIL**   1.1 mi. • Moderate • 1 hr.   Date:______

This trail offers one of the best views of mesquite trees in the park. While native to Texas and highly drought-tolerant, mesquite can spread aggressively in some areas, where it competes with grasses.

Trail Notes: _______________________________________________

_______________________________________________

_______________________________________________

☐ **OTTINE SWAMP TRAIL**   1.0 mi. • Moderate • 1 hr.   Date:______

Named for the nearby town of Ottine, this trail winds past seasonal swamps.

Trail Notes: _______________________________________________

_______________________________________________

_______________________________________________

☐ **SAN MARCOS RIVER TRAIL**   1.3 mi. • Moderate • 1.5 hrs.   Date:______

This trail follows much of the San Marcos River and offers excellent wildlife viewing, especially for birdwatchers.

Trail Notes: _______________________________________________

_______________________________________________

_______________________________________________

# Palmetto State Park

☐ **MOSSYCUP SPUR**       0.3 mi. •       Easy       • 30 min.       Date:_________

Watch for the bur oak's oversized acorns—the largest native to North America—measuring up to about 1½ inches. Their fringed cups give them the nickname "mossy cup."

Trail Notes: _______________________________________________

_______________________________________________

_______________________________________________

☐ **PARK HQ TRAIL**       0.2 mi. •       Easy       • 30 min.       Date:_________

This short trail leads to the park's day-use and tent camping areas, with options to kayak, paddleboard, fish, or stay overnight in a cabin.

Trail Notes: _______________________________________________

_______________________________________________

_______________________________________________

☐ **LOW WATER CROSSING PATH**       0.1 mi.                     Date:_________

Trail Notes: _______________________________________________

_______________________________________________

_______________________________________________

## ⚲ Trailward Finds

☐ **OXBOW LAKE**
DATE:

☐ **ARTESIAN WELL**
DATE:

☐ **LOW-WATER CROSSING**
DATE:

☐ **CCC REFECTORY**
DATE:

☐ **EXTINCT MUD BOILS**
DATE:

☐ **CCC WATER TOWER**
DATE:

Park Website       Trail Map

Visit the Texas Parks & Wildlife
Department at tpwd.texas.gov

# Pedernales Falls State Park

☐ **HACKENBURG LOOP**    1.4 mi. • Moderate • 1 hr.    Date:__________

Named after an early landowning family, this rugged trail follows the river through areas shaped by past flash floods.

Trail Notes: ______________________________________________

______________________________________________

______________________________________________

☐ **TWIN FALLS NATURE TRAIL**    0.5 mi. (round trip) • Moderate • 30 min.    Date:__________

This short, rugged trail leads to one of the Hill Country's most scenic destinations.

Trail Notes: ______________________________________________

______________________________________________

______________________________________________

☐ **PEDERNALES FALLS TRAIL SYSTEM**    0.3 – 1.8 mi. • Moderate • 1 hr.    Date:__________

Spend an hour or a full day exploring the dramatic rock formations around Pedernales Falls, with options to extend your hike along connecting side trails.

Trail Notes: ______________________________________________

______________________________________________

______________________________________________

☐ **CYPRESS MILL LOOP**    4.9 mi. • Moderate • 3.5 hrs.    Date:__________

Expect wet feet when crossing the river at Trammell Crossing to reach a historic area of the park with scenic views.

Trail Notes: ______________________________________________

______________________________________________

______________________________________________

☐ **WOLF MOUNTAIN LOOP**    5.5 mi. (round trip) • Moderate • 3 hrs.    Date:__________

Named for the "prairie wolf," or coyote, the Wolf Mountain Loop features scenic overlooks, cool springs, and winding Hill Country creeks.

Trail Notes: ______________________________________________

______________________________________________

______________________________________________

# Pedernales Falls State Park

☐ JONES SPRING TRAIL   2.6 mi. • Moderate • 1.5 hr   Date:___________

This trail winds through dense cedar forest to Jones Spring and the remains of a historic rock house.

Trail Notes: ____________________________________________

____________________________________________

____________________________________________


☐ JUNIPER RIDGE TRAIL  9.7 mi. • Challenging •  6 hrs.   Date:___________

This shaded trail is ideal for technical single-track biking or a full day of hiking.

Trail Notes: ____________________________________________

____________________________________________

____________________________________________


☐ MADRONE TRAIL        4.3 mi. • Moderate • 2.5 hrs.   Date:___________

Named for its madrone trees—rare in the Texas Hill Country—this trail requires caution when crossing the county road.

Trail Notes: ____________________________________________

____________________________________________

____________________________________________


☐ HORSE TRAIL – NORTH        2.5 mi. •    Easy    • 1.5 hrs.   Date:___________

This easy trail welcomes hikers, bikers, and horseback riders, with frequent wildlife drawn to nearby food and water sources.

Trail Notes: ____________________________________________

____________________________________________

____________________________________________


☐ HORSE TRAIL – SOUTH        11.4 mi. • Moderate • 8 hrs.   Date:___________

Travel through rugged limestone hills on foot, horseback, or mountain bike, with connections to other trails for a longer outing.

Trail Notes: ____________________________________________

____________________________________________

____________________________________________

*Continued on next page*   

# Pedernales Falls State Park

☐ WINDMILL ROAD          0.6 mi.                    Date:________

Trail Notes: __________________________________________

______________________________________________________

______________________________________________________

☐ WHEATLEY TRAIL          0.7 mi.                    Date:________

Trail Notes: __________________________________________

______________________________________________________

______________________________________________________

☐ WARFLE'S TRAIL          0.4 mi.                    Date:________

Trail Notes: __________________________________________

______________________________________________________

______________________________________________________

☐ COYOTE CROSSING          0.3 mi.                    Date:________

Trail Notes: __________________________________________

______________________________________________________

______________________________________________________

## 📍 Trailward Finds

☐ TRAMMELL CROSSING
DATE:

☐ TWIN FALLS OVERLOOK
DATE:

☐ STAR THEATER / BIRD BLIND
DATE:

☐ JONES SPRING
DATE:

☐ HILL COUNTRY/RIVER OVERLOOKS
DATE:

☐ PEDERNALES FALLS/CYPRESS POOL OVERLOOK
DATE:

Park Website          Trail Map

Visit the Texas Parks & Wildlife
Department at tpwd.texas.gov

# South Llano River State Park

☐ INTERPRETIVE TRAIL   0.4 mi. •   Easy   • 25 min.   Date:__________

Enjoy a shaded walk through bottomland hardwood forest featuring cedar elm, pecan, and several oak species, including chinquapin, live, red, and shin oak.

Trail Notes: ________________________________________________
________________________________________________
________________________________________________

☐ BUCK LAKE TRAIL   1.6 mi. •   Easy   • 1 hr.   Date:__________

Named for the family who donated the land, this oxbow lake was once part of the South Llano River. Watch for resident beavers, and note that the nearest parking is about 50 yards down the road.

Trail Notes: ________________________________________________
________________________________________________
________________________________________________

☐ RIVER TRAIL   1.6 mi. •   Easy   • 1 hr.   Date:__________

Follow the spring-fed South Llano River while watching for wildlife, then continue into a bottomland hardwood forest filled with diverse trees.

Trail Notes: ________________________________________________
________________________________________________
________________________________________________

☐ OVERLOOK TRAIL   0.9 mi. • Moderate • 45 min.   Date:__________
(one way)

For sweeping views, park near the walk-in campsites and hike a short, steep climb to a scenic overlook. Bikes are not allowed due to the grade.

Trail Notes: ________________________________________________
________________________________________________
________________________________________________

☐ FAWN TRAIL   1.3 mi. • Moderate • 1 hr.   Date:__________

This trail shifts from bottomland to upland terrain, offering a chance to observe changing plant and animal life along the way.

Trail Notes: ________________________________________________
________________________________________________
________________________________________________

*Continued on next page*   

# South Llano River State Park

☐ **MID-CANYON TRAIL**    2.5 mi. • Moderate • 1.5 hrs.    Date:_________

With more than 250 bird species recorded—including the endangered golden-cheeked warbler—this backcountry trail also offers chances to see porcupines, skunks, ringtails, and white-tailed deer. Move quietly for the best wildlife sightings.

Trail Notes: ______________________________________________

___________________________________________________________

___________________________________________________________

☐ **WEST CANYON LOOP TRAIL**    2.4 mi. • Moderate • 1.5 hrs.    Date:_________

This trail passes through a canyon, crosses a plateau, and then descends steeply through dense Ashe juniper and hardwood forest.

Trail Notes: ______________________________________________

___________________________________________________________

___________________________________________________________

☐ **FRONTERA TRAIL**    4.0 mi. • Moderate to Difficult • 2.5 hrs.    Date:_________

Ideal for long hikes or mountain bike rides, this backcountry route follows the park boundary with elevated views, winding single-track, and a quiet, remote feel.

Trail Notes: ______________________________________________

___________________________________________________________

___________________________________________________________

☐ **EAST RIDGE TRAIL**    2.8 mi. • Moderate • 2 hrs.    Date:_________

This mountain biking trail offers views along the edge of the Hill Country.

Trail Notes: ______________________________________________

___________________________________________________________

___________________________________________________________

☐ **UPPER RIVER TRAIL**    0.3 mi.    Date:_________

Trail Notes: ______________________________________________

___________________________________________________________

___________________________________________________________

# South Llano River State Park

☐ WALTER'S WAY    0.6 mi.                    Date:

Trail Notes: ________________________________________

______________________________________________________

______________________________________________________


☐ TURKEY ROOST TRAIL  1.6 mi.               Date:

Trail Notes: ________________________________________

______________________________________________________

______________________________________________________


☐ WEST FIELD TRAIL    1.0 mi.               Date:

Trail Notes: ________________________________________

______________________________________________________

______________________________________________________


☐ AGARITA TRAIL    0.4 mi.                  Date:

Trail Notes: ________________________________________

______________________________________________________

______________________________________________________


☐ PRICKLY PEAR SPUR
   TRAIL          0.3 mi.                   Date:

Trail Notes: ________________________________________

______________________________________________________

______________________________________________________


☐ WINDMILL HILL
   TRAIL          0.8 mi.                   Date:

Trail Notes: ________________________________________

______________________________________________________

______________________________________________________


☐ BUCK'S SHORTCUT    0.5 mi.                Date:

Trail Notes: ________________________________________

______________________________________________________

______________________________________________________


☐ DOUBLE LOOP 1    0.7 mi.                  Date:

Trail Notes: ________________________________________

______________________________________________________

______________________________________________________

*Continued on next page*   

# South Llano River State Park

☐ DOUBLE LOOP 2          0.4 mi.                    Date:

Trail Notes: _______________________________________________

_______________________________________________

_______________________________________________

☐ TURKEY SPUR TRAIL      0.1 mi.                    Date:

Trail Notes: _______________________________________________

_______________________________________________

_______________________________________________

## 📍 Trailward Finds

☐ **BUCK LAKE**
DATE:

☐ **SCENIC OVERLOOK**
DATE:

☐ **CANYON SEEP**
DATE:

☐ **WINDMILL**
DATE:

☐ **OLD BARN**
DATE:

☐ **BUCK HOUSE, CEMETERY AND OUTBUILDINGS**
DATE:

Park Website          Trail Map

Visit the Texas Parks & Wildlife
Department at tpwd.texas.gov

# WEST TEXAS
## R E G I O N

| TRAILS TO EXPLORE | PARKS INCLUDED |
| --- | --- |
| 171 | 21 |

## Regional Milestones

☐ First Park Completed

Trail: ___________________

Date: ___________________

☐ Final Park Completed

Trail: ___________________

Date: ___________________

☐ Favorite Trail

Trail: ___________________

Date: ___________________

☐ Longest Trail Completed

12-Mile Loop

Date: ___________________

☐ Shortest Trail Completed

Site 19 Trail

Date: ___________________

☐ Most Challenging Trail Completed

Trail: ___________________

Date: ___________________

## All **171** West Texas Trails Completed

336.59 Miles Hiked

Date: ___________________          Total Miles Hiked: ___________________

# Abilene State Park

☐ ABILENE DAM ROAD   3.5 mi. • Moderate   Date:__________

This scenic loop overlooks Lake Abilene and Elm Creek Valley—bring plenty of water. Watch for roadrunners and white-tailed deer in the hills, with waterfowl and beavers near the lake.

Trail Notes: __________________________________________

______________________________________________________

______________________________________________________

☐ BIRD TRAIL   0.3 mi. •   Easy   Date:__________

Once a CCC road, this trail now leads hikers to the bird blind.

Trail Notes: __________________________________________

______________________________________________________

______________________________________________________

☐ LEGACY TRAIL   0.2 mi. •   Easy   Date:__________

This short historic walk highlights the CCC's legacy and the importance of leaving artifacts where they are. Once a route to a former campground, the trail still features remnants of CCC-built structures.

Trail Notes: __________________________________________

______________________________________________________

______________________________________________________

☐ BUFFALO WALLOW NATURE TRAIL   0.2 mi. •   Easy   Date:__________

Walk the loop around this spring-fed pond, a prime spot for observing local amphibians and reptiles.

Trail Notes: __________________________________________

______________________________________________________

______________________________________________________

☐ CONNECTING TRAIL   0.1 mi. •   Easy   Date:__________

This CCC-built trail provides an off-road connection between the Elm Creek Nature Trail and the Bird Trail.

Trail Notes: __________________________________________

______________________________________________________

______________________________________________________

# Abilene State Park

☐ EAGLE TRAIL  0.2 mi. • Easy  Date:_________
(ADA Accessible)

As you pass the park's water tower, look up for vultures that often roost there. Trailside benches offer easy spots to pause and enjoy the view.

Trail Notes: _________________________________________________

_________________________________________________________________

_________________________________________________________________

☐ ELM CREEK NATURE TRAIL  0.9 mi. • Easy  Date:_________

This scenic loop winds through the park beneath towering elm, pecan, oak, and black willow trees.

Trail Notes: _________________________________________________

_________________________________________________________________

_________________________________________________________________

☐ OAK GROVE TRAIL  0.2 mi. • Easy  Date:_________

Following Elm Creek, this CCC-built trail is a great place to spot wildlife tracks near the water.

Trail Notes: _________________________________________________

_________________________________________________________________

_________________________________________________________________

## 📍 Trailward Finds

☐ COWBOY CIRCLE
DATE:

☐ BIRD VIEWING BLIND
DATE:

☐ BUFFALO WALLOW
DATE:

☐ FISHING DOCK
DATE:

☐ BACK BOAT RAMP
DATE:

☐ LAKE PICNIC/SWIMMING AREA
DATE:

☐ CCC WATER TOWER AND PLAYGROUND
DATE:

☐ CCC CONCESSION BUILDING AND SWIMMING POOL
DATE:

Park Website    Trail Map
Visit the Texas Parks & Wildlife
Department at tpwd.texas.gov

# Balmorhea State Park

This state park centers around its iconic spring-fed pool rather than an extensive trail system. We've included space for notes about the pool and surrounding features. No **Trail Map** is available for this park.

☐ SPRING FED SWIMMING POOL                      Date:_________

Landmark Notes: ______________________________________________

______________________________________________________________

______________________________________________________________

______________________________________________________________

☐ RECONSTRUCTED DESERT WETLANDS                      Date:_________

Landmark Notes: ______________________________________________

______________________________________________________________

______________________________________________________________

______________________________________________________________

☐ HUBBS CIÉNEGA                      Date:_________

Landmark Notes: ______________________________________________

______________________________________________________________

______________________________________________________________

______________________________________________________________

☐ SAN SOLOMON SPRINGS OVERLOOK                      Date:_________

Landmark Notes: ______________________________________________

______________________________________________________________

______________________________________________________________

______________________________________________________________

Park Website        Park Map

Visit the Texas Parks & Wildlife
Department at tpwd.texas.gov

# Barton Warnock Visitor Center

This visitor center doesn't have its own trails, so space is provided for notes instead of a trail map.
No **Trail Map** for this park.

☐      Date:__________

Landmark Notes: ________________________________

_____________________________________________

_____________________________________________

_____________________________________________

☐      Date:__________

Landmark Notes: ________________________________

_____________________________________________

_____________________________________________

_____________________________________________

## 📍 Trailward Finds

☐ DATE:

☐ DATE:

☐ DATE:

☐ DATE:

☐ DATE:

☐ DATE:

Park Website     Complex Map

Visit the Texas Parks & Wildlife
Department at tpwd.texas.gov

# Big Bend Ranch State Park

Big Bend Ranch State Park features an extensive trail system, with individual PDF maps available for each trail. QR code to **Trail Maps** are located next to the trails.

☐ **CLOSED CANYON TRAIL**  1.4 mi.    Date: ___________

Closed Canyon is a narrow slot canyon carved through Colorado Mesa, formed millions of years ago from volcanic rock and shaped by erosion and flash flooding. There is no defined trail—the towering canyon walls guide the route as it narrows toward the Rio Grande, with smooth, polished rock, sand, and gravel underfoot. Shaded conditions keep the canyon cooler than the surrounding desert and support wildlife, desert plants, and fragile tinajas that collect water and should be left undisturbed. Flash flooding and slick rock are serious hazards, so always check conditions and use caution while hiking.

Trail Notes:_______________________________________________

_____________________________________________________________

_____________________________________________________________

☐ **CINCO TINAJAS TRAIL**  0.5 mi. •  Easy    Date:___________

☐ **LEYVA ESCONDIDO LOOP TRAIL**  3.1 mi. • Challenging    Date:___________

Cinco Tinajas, meaning "five pools," is located about 1.3 miles west of Sauceda Headquarters and features five water-filled rock basins that hold water most of the year, supporting desert plants and wildlife. Hikers can choose a short, easy walk to the tinajas or a longer, more challenging loop to Leyva Escondido Spring with steep climbs, deep sand, and sweeping views. The area is best suited for hiking and horseback riding—mountain biking is not recommended—and visitors should watch for wildlife, bring plenty of water, and use caution around slick rock and sensitive tinaja habitats.

Trail Notes:_______________________________________________

_____________________________________________________________

_____________________________________________________________

## 📍 Trailward Finds

☐ CINCO TINAJAS OVERLOOK
DATE:

☐ ROCK ART
DATE:

# Big Bend Ranch State Park

Big Bend Ranch State Park features an extensive trail system, with individual PDF maps available for each trail.
QR code to **Trail Maps** are located next to the trails.

## The Contrabando Multi-Use Trail System

The Contrabando Multi-Use Trail System includes roughly 25 miles of interconnected wagon roads and single-track trails originally shaped by ranchers, stage routes, and cinnabar prospectors from the late 1800s through the mid-1900s. Once key travel corridors linking Presidio, Lajitas, Terlingua, and surrounding ranches, many of these routes were abandoned after FM 170 was completed along the Rio Grande. Today, the trail system offers sweeping desert views, hidden canyons, evolving geology, and historic sites—please travel responsibly to help preserve this landscape for future visitors.

☐ EAST MAIN TRAIL    8.5 mi. •    Easy    Date:__________

Trail Notes: __________________________________________

___________________________________________________________

___________________________________________________________

☐ WEST MAIN TRAIL    5.0 mi. •  Difficult    Date:__________

Trail Notes: __________________________________________

___________________________________________________________

___________________________________________________________

☐ CAMINO VIEJO TRAIL    1.2 mi. •  Moderate    Date:__________

Trail Notes: __________________________________________

___________________________________________________________

___________________________________________________________

☐ CONTRABANDISTA SPUR    0.6 mi. •    Easy    Date:__________

Trail Notes: __________________________________________

___________________________________________________________

___________________________________________________________

☐ CRYSTAL TRAIL    1.3 mi. •  Moderate    Date:__________

Trail Notes: __________________________________________

___________________________________________________________

___________________________________________________________

☐ DOG CHOLLA TRAIL    1.4 mi. •  Moderate    Date:__________

Trail Notes: __________________________________________

___________________________________________________________

___________________________________________________________

# Big Bend Ranch State Park

Big Bend Ranch State Park features an extensive trail system, with individual PDF maps available for each trail.
QR code to **Trail Maps** are located next to the trails.

## The Contrabando Multi-Use Trail System

☐ DOME TRAIL          4.0 mi.  •  Difficult          Date:___________

Trail Notes: _______________________________________________

_______________________________________________

_______________________________________________

☐ ROCK QUARRY TRAIL   1.0 mi.  •  Moderate          Date:___________

Trail Notes: _______________________________________________

_______________________________________________

_______________________________________________

## 📍 Trailward Finds

☐ CINNABAR PROSPECT
DATE:

☐ CINNABAR MINE
DATE:

☐ CONTRABANDO WATERHOLE
DATE:

☐ CANDELILLA WAX CAMP
DATE:

# Big Bend Ranch State Park

Big Bend Ranch State Park features an extensive trail system, with individual PDF maps available for each trail.
QR code to **Trail Maps** are located next to the trails.

☐ ENCINO TRAIL          7.2 mi.                    Date: __________

Encino Loop Trail is a 7.2-mile loop east of Sauceda Ranger Station, featuring a mix of single-track, double-track, and dirt road through rolling hills, mesas, and Chihuahuan Desert grasslands. The route is popular with mountain bikers for its fast, flowing terrain, with some rocky sections and deep sand, while hikers and equestrians are also welcome. Visible landmarks like La Mota Mesa help with navigation, and riding from Sauceda Ranger Station adds mileage for a longer, more challenging outing.

Trail Notes:_______________________________________________

_______________________________________________

_______________________________________________

☐ HORSETRAP TRAIL       4.3 mi.                    Date: __________

Horsetrap Trail is a 4.3-mile loop near Sauceda Ranger Station, combining old double-track and single-track with gentle grades and wide views of rolling hills and low mesas. Named for nearby Horsetrap Springs, the route crosses historic ranch pastureland and is suitable for hiking, horseback riding, and mountain biking, with counterclockwise travel recommended for cyclists due to loose rock and sandy sections. The trail is shared by multiple user groups, so yield as needed, watch for wildlife, and carry plenty of water.

Trail Notes:_______________________________________________

_______________________________________________

_______________________________________________

☐ SAUCEDA NATURE TRAIL       0.9 mi. • Easy                    Date: __________

Sauceda Nature Trail is an easy 0.9-mile loop just south of the Sauceda complex, crossing desert grassland, shrubs, and succulents typical of the Chihuahuan Desert. The route climbs a rocky lava ridge similar to formations in the Bofecillos Mountains and has little maintained tread. Interpretive signs highlight common plants, and the hilltop offers some of the best views of La Mota Mountain and the historic Sauceda complex.

Trail Notes:_______________________________________________

_______________________________________________

_______________________________________________

*Continued on next page*   

# Big Bend Ranch State Park

Big Bend Ranch State Park features an extensive trail system, with individual PDF maps available for each trail.
QR code to **Trail Maps** are located next to the trails.

☐ **FRESNO DIVIDE TRAIL** — 6.5 mi. (round trip) — Date: _________

Fresno Divide Trail is a 3.2-mile segment of the Contrabando Multi-Use Trail System, following the divide between Fresno and Contrabando creeks and offering expansive desert views and historic landscapes. Open to hikers, mountain bikers, and equestrians, the trail is easy on foot but more challenging for cyclists due to climbs, rocky sections, and drainage crossings. Starting from the West Contrabando Trailhead, the hike to the overlook is a 6.5-mile round trip—bring water, watch for wildlife, and yield to other users as needed.

Trail Notes:_______________________________________________

_______________________________________________

_______________________________________________

☐ **HOODOOS TRAIL** — 1.0 mi. — Date: _________

Hoodoos Trail is an easy hike along River Road (FM 170), where unusual rock formations shaped by wind and water rise above views of the Rio Grande and Mexico. The route follows part of a historic road once used by early travelers and border patrols, offering close-up geology and scenic overlooks right from the trailhead. Although hoodoos may look solid, they are fragile—bring water, watch for wildlife, check conditions, and avoid climbing on the formations to help protect them.

Trail Notes:_______________________________________________

_______________________________________________

_______________________________________________

☐ **OJITO ADENTRO TRAIL** — 0.4 mi. • Easy — Date: _________

Ojito Adentro Trail is a short 0.4-mile hike in the Bofecillos Mountains leading to lush springs and a seasonal waterfall known as "little spring within." Because water is present most of the year, this area supports rich plant and animal life and is one of the park's top birding spots—bring binoculars and stay out of the sensitive spring waters. Always carry water, watch for wildlife, and check with park rangers about trail and weather conditions before hiking.

Trail Notes:_______________________________________________

_______________________________________________

_______________________________________________

# Big Spring State Park

☐ **NATURE TRAIL**    0.4 mi. •    Easy    • 45 min.    Date:______________

This one-way descent showcases the meeting point of three distinct ecosystems as it drops from the mountain to the lower park road.

Trail Notes: ______________________________________________

______________________________________________

______________________________________________

☐ **SCENIC MOUNTAIN LOOP**    4.0 mi. •  Moderate  •  2 hrs.    Date:______________

This loop around Scenic Mountain offers a moderate challenge for hikers and bikers, along with wide views of the surrounding terrain.

Trail Notes: ______________________________________________

______________________________________________

______________________________________________

☐ **OUTER LIMITS TRAIL**   1.2 mi. •  Challenging  •   1 hr.    Date:______________

Extend your Scenic Mountain Loop hike by taking this more remote, off-the-beaten-path route.

Trail Notes: ______________________________________________

______________________________________________

______________________________________________

☐ **SOTOL STROLL LOOP**   0.6 mi. •    Easy    • 30 min.    Date:______________

This easy walk near the lower parking lot is home to the park's only sotol plant.

Trail Notes: ______________________________________________

______________________________________________

______________________________________________

## ⦿ Trailward Finds

☐ **CCC ROMAN ROAD**
DATE:

☐ **CCC PUMPHOUSE**
DATE:

☐ **CCC ROCK QUARRY**
DATE:

☐ **HISTORIC CARVINGS**
DATE:

Park Website     Trail Map
Visit the Texas Parks & Wildlife
Department at tpwd.texas.gov

# Davis Mountains State Park

☐ **HEADQUARTERS TRAIL** — 0.3 mi. (one way) • Easy • 10–15 min. Date:_________

This easy scenic walk offers views of Keesey Canyon below and an ancient lava flow above, ending at the Emory Oak Wildlife Viewing Area.

Trail Notes: _______________________________________________

_______________________________________________

_______________________________________________

☐ **MONTEZUMA QUAIL TRAIL** — 0.9 mi. (one way) • Moderate – Challenging • 1 hr. Date:_________

From the wildlife viewing area, a quick 220-foot climb leads to canyon and Indian Lodge views, followed by a brief ridge walk and a steep descent to the campground.

Trail Notes: _______________________________________________

_______________________________________________

_______________________________________________

☐ **INDIAN LODGE TRAIL** — 1.5 mi. (one way) • Challenging • 1.5 hrs. Date:_________

Starting behind Indian Lodge, this trail climbs to sweeping views of the Davis Mountains, then connects with the Montezuma Quail Trail to return to the campground or continue on to headquarters.

Trail Notes: _______________________________________________

_______________________________________________

_______________________________________________

☐ **SKYLINE DRIVE TRAIL** — 2.6 mi. (one way) • Moderate – Challenging • 2 hrs. Date:_________

From the Interpretive Center, climb 544 feet to Keesey Canyon Overlook, then follow Skyline Drive past historic structures and views of Fort Davis before ending at the CCC trailhead.

Trail Notes: _______________________________________________

_______________________________________________

_______________________________________________

☐ **LIMPIA CREEK TRAIL** — 2.4 mi. (one way) • Moderate – Challenging • 2 hrs. Date:_________

From the parking lot, an easy, level path through Limpia Canyon leads into a gradual 550-foot climb to the Sheep Pen Canyon Loop junction, with sweeping views of the Davis Mountains along the way.

Trail Notes: _______________________________________________

_______________________________________________

_______________________________________________

# Davis Mountains State Park

☐ **SHEEP PEN CANYON LOOP**  5.6 mi. • Moderate • 3-4 hrs.  Date:_________

Cross a mountain plateau through oak-juniper forest and high desert grasslands, with some of the park's best views. Look for a historic well and side trails leading to primitive campsites and Limpia Creek Vista.

Trail Notes: _________________________________________________

_________________________________________________

_________________________________________________

☐ **OLD CCC TRAIL**  1.6 mi. (one way) • Moderate • 1.5 hr.  Date:_________

This former CCC construction road from the 1930s now serves as a hiking trail, with connections at the top to the Skyline Drive and Fort Trails.

Trail Notes: _________________________________________________

_________________________________________________

_________________________________________________

☐ **Vista Trail**  0.3 mi.  Date:_________

Trail Notes: _________________________________________________

_________________________________________________

_________________________________________________

# 📍 Trailward Finds

☐ **SKYLINE DRIVE**
DATE:

☐ **THE KING'S TABLE**
DATE:

☐ **KEESEY CANYON OVERLOOK**
DATE:

☐ **TRAILHEAD TO FORT DAVIS NATIONAL HISTORIC SITE**
DATE:

☐ **INTERPRETIVE CENTER**
DATE:

☐ **INDIAN LODGE**
DATE:

☐ **EMORY OAK WILDLIFE VIEWING AREA**
DATE:

☐ **HEADQUARTERS TRAIL**
DATE:

☐ **LIMPIA CREEK VISTA**
DATE:

Park Website    Trail Map

Visit the Texas Parks & Wildlife
Department at tpwd.texas.gov

☐ **KENNARD CANYON TRAIL**   2.0 mi. • Challenging     Date:__________

Starting at Devils Back Campground, this rolling out-and-back trail leads into Kennard Canyon. Watch for Devils Tower, a striking rock monolith that glows in the evening summer sun.

Trail Notes: ________________________________________________

____________________________________________________________

____________________________________________________________

☐ **LITTLE SATAN TRAIL**   3.8 mi. • Challenging     Date:__________

This gradual descent leads into Little Satan Canyon, where thornscrub transitions into oak and juniper woodlands. The trail ends at the river beneath towering sycamore trees.

Trail Notes: ________________________________________________

____________________________________________________________

____________________________________________________________

☐ **LITTLE SATAN SPUR**   0.9 mi. • Moderate     Date:__________

This spur provides a convenient parking access for backpackers heading into Little Satan Canyon. Use caution, as the trail includes steep sections.

Trail Notes: ________________________________________________

____________________________________________________________

____________________________________________________________

☐ **OVERLOOK TRAIL**   2.1 mi. • Moderate     Date:__________

This rolling ridgeline hike leads to sweeping views of the Devils River, known for its aquamarine waters fed by karst springs. Over time, erosion has carved the riverbed into deep channels that support unique habitats.

Trail Notes: ________________________________________________

____________________________________________________________

____________________________________________________________

☐ **GAGE CANYON TRAIL**   2.7 mi. • Challenging     Date:__________

This wandering trail crosses the canyon multiple times, with a great stopping point at the Gage Tinajas.

Trail Notes: ________________________________________________

____________________________________________________________

____________________________________________________________

# Devils River State Natural Area

## Dan A. Hughes Unit

☐ GAGE CANYON SPUR    0.4 mi.  •  Moderate                    Date:________

This spur allows hikers to complete a loop from Gage Canyon Trail by returning along the main park road. Keep an eye out for bobwhite and scaled quail along the ridge.

Trail Notes: _______________________________________________

_______________________________________________________

_______________________________________________________

## 📍 Trailward Finds

☐ GARDEN OF THE TRI-ECOREGIONS
DATE:

☐ GAGE GANYON TINAJAS
DATE:

☐ DEVILS RIVER OVERLOOK
DATE:

☐ DEVILS TOWER
DATE:

Park Website        Trail Map

Visit the Texas Parks & Wildlife
Department at tpwd.texas.gov

# Devils River State Natural Area

## Del Norte Unit

☐ NEWTON LOOP  0.1 mi. • Easy  Date:__________

This trail features two wildlife blinds along a native plant path often filled with cactus wren songs. Remnants of historic ranching structures from the Newton family can still be seen in the area.

Trail Notes: _______________________________________

_______________________________________

_______________________________________

☐ 12-MILE LOOP  12.4 mi. • Challenging  Date:__________

Take in sweeping landscape views while passing historic ranching structures once used by the Fawcett family.

Trail Notes: _______________________________________

_______________________________________

_______________________________________

☐ 5-MILE LOOP  5.0 mi. • Challenging  Date:__________

Choose this shorter route instead of the full 12-mile loop to explore the diverse plant life of Devils River SNA.

Trail Notes: _______________________________________

_______________________________________

_______________________________________

☐ FIREBREAK TRAIL  3.7 mi. • Challenging  Date:__________

Expansive backcountry canyon views reward hikers on this trail designed to help protect natural resources.

Trail Notes: _______________________________________

_______________________________________

_______________________________________

☐ FINEGAN SPRINGS TRAIL  1.4 mi. • Moderate  Date:__________

Follow the river with care as the trail crosses the waters of Finegan Springs. This lush oasis supports abundant wildlife and excellent birdwatching beneath the riverside canopy.

Trail Notes: _______________________________________

_______________________________________

_______________________________________

# Devils River State Natural Area

## Del Norte Unit

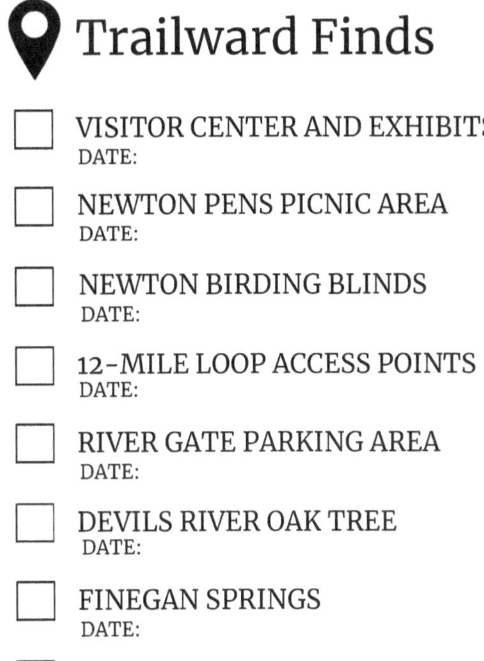

## Trailward Finds

Park Website    Trail Map

Visit the Texas Parks & Wildlife
Department at tpwd.texas.gov

- ☐ VISITOR CENTER AND EXHIBITS
  DATE:

- ☐ NEWTON PENS PICNIC AREA
  DATE:

- ☐ NEWTON BIRDING BLINDS
  DATE:

- ☐ 12-MILE LOOP ACCESS POINTS
  DATE:

- ☐ RIVER GATE PARKING AREA
  DATE:

- ☐ DEVILS RIVER OAK TREE
  DATE:

- ☐ FINEGAN SPRINGS
  DATE:

- ☐ WINDMILL
  DATE:

# Devil's Sinkhole State Natural Area

This Texas State Park is **reservation only**, and official trail or park maps are **not** available. We've included space here to help you track trails, landmarks, mileage, and discoveries during your visit.

Date:__________

Trail Notes: __________________________________________

__________________________________________

__________________________________________

__________________________________________

Date:__________

Trail Notes: __________________________________________

__________________________________________

__________________________________________

__________________________________________

Date:__________

Trail Notes: __________________________________________

__________________________________________

__________________________________________

__________________________________________

## Trailward Finds

DATE:

DATE:

DATE:

DATE:

DATE:

**Park Website**

Visit the Texas Parks & Wildlife Department at tpwd.texas.gov

# Fort Leaton State Historic Site

This state park emphasizes historical landmarks over hiking trails. To match that experience, we've provided space for notes on the park's historical sites instead of a trail map.

☐ FORT LEATON STATE HISTORIC SITE                    Date:__________

Landmark Notes: _______________________________________________

_____________________________________________________________

_____________________________________________________________

_____________________________________________________________

## 📍 Trailward Finds

☐ SERVANTS' QUARTERS 1, 2 AND 3

☐ FORMAL PARLOR

☐ NURSERY/FORMAL SITTING ROOM

☐ FAMILY PARLOR

☐ TRADING OFFICE

☐ DINING ROOM

☐ COURTYARD

☐ KITCHEN

☐ PANTRY

☐ CARRETAS ON THE CHIHUAHUA TRAIL

☐ THE BAKERY

☐ GUARDROOM AND "DUNGEON"

☐ BLACKSMITH SHOP

☐ UNRESTORED ROOMS

☐ GRANARY

☐ MAUSOLEUM AND CEMETERY

☐ EXHIBITS

**Park Website**     **Site Map**

Visit the Texas Parks & Wildlife
Department at tpwd.texas.gov

# Franklin Mountains State Park

## Tom Mays Unit

☐ SCHAEFFER SHUFFLE   2.6 mi.                    Date:__________

Trail Notes: ______________________________________________

_________________________________________________________

_________________________________________________________

☐ UPPER SUNSET   1.3 mi.                    Date:__________

Trail Notes: ______________________________________________

_________________________________________________________

_________________________________________________________

☐ LOWER SUNSET   3.6 mi.                    Date:__________

Trail Notes: ______________________________________________

_________________________________________________________

_________________________________________________________

☐ TOM MAYS TRAIL                    Date:__________

Trail Notes: ______________________________________________

_________________________________________________________

_________________________________________________________

☐ NATURE WALK   0.75 mi.                    Date:__________

Trail Notes: ______________________________________________

_________________________________________________________

_________________________________________________________

☐ LOOP 1   2.3 mi.                    Date:__________

Trail Notes: ______________________________________________

_________________________________________________________

_________________________________________________________

☐ LOOP 2   1.3 mi.                    Date:__________

Trail Notes: ______________________________________________

_________________________________________________________

_________________________________________________________

☐ LOOP 3   2.3 mi.                    Date:__________

Trail Notes: ______________________________________________

_________________________________________________________

_________________________________________________________

# Franklin Mountains State Park

## Tom Mays Unit

☐ LOOP 4          1.5 mi.          Date:__________

Trail Notes: _______________________________________

_______________________________________

_______________________________________

☐ LOOP 5          0.5 mi.          Date:__________

Trail Notes: _______________________________________

_______________________________________

_______________________________________

☐ LOOP 6          4.0 mi.          Date:__________

Trail Notes: _______________________________________

_______________________________________

_______________________________________

☐ AZTEC CAVES          1.9 mi.          Date:__________

Trail Notes: _______________________________________

_______________________________________

_______________________________________

☐ MUNDY'S GAP          4.0 mi.          Date:__________

Trail Notes: _______________________________________

_______________________________________

_______________________________________

☐ N. FRANKLIN PEAK          7.8 mi.          Date:__________
(round trip)

Trail Notes: _______________________________________

_______________________________________

_______________________________________

☐ W. COTTONWOOD SPRING          1.6 mi.          Date:__________
(round trip)

Trail Notes: _______________________________________

_______________________________________

_______________________________________

☐ AGAVE LOOP          1.3 mi.          Date:__________

Trail Notes: _______________________________________

_______________________________________

_______________________________________

Continued on next page    

# Franklin Mountains State Park

## Tom Mays Unit

☐ W. COTTONWOOD
SPRING SCENIC ROUTE    2.9 mi.
(round trip)    Date:__________

Trail Notes: _______________________________________

_______________________________________

_______________________________________

☐ BEGINNER'S LOOP    1.2 mi.    Date:__________

Trail Notes: _______________________________________

_______________________________________

_______________________________________

## 📍 Trailward Finds

☐ SNEED'S CORY
DATE:

☐ MUNDY'S GAP
DATE:

☐ AZTEC CAVES
DATE:

☐ SCENIC OVERLOOK
DATE:

☐ WILDLIFE VIEWING
DATE:

☐ AMPHITHEATER
DATE:

☐ N. FRANKLIN PEAK
DATE:

Park Website     Park Map

Visit the Texas Parks & Wildlife
Department at tpwd.texas.gov

# Government Canyon State Natural Area

☐ **SAVANNAH LOOP**     2.6 mi. •     Easy     • 1 –1.5 hrs.   Date:___________
(round trip)

This loop starts and finishes at the Frontcountry Trailhead and is ideal for a relaxed walk with kids or dogs.

Trail Notes: _______________________________________________

_______________________________________________

_______________________________________________

☐ **LYTLE'S LOOP**     5.0 mi. •     Easy –     • 2.5 – 3.5   Date:___________
(round trip)     Moderate     hrs.

This loop begins and ends at the Frontcountry Trailhead and offers chances to spot wildlife such as Rio Grande wild turkey, northern bobwhite quail, and white-tailed deer in the surrounding savannah.

Trail Notes: _______________________________________________

_______________________________________________

_______________________________________________

☐ **NORTH BLUFF SPURS OVERLOOK**     3.4 mi. • Moderate • 1.5 – 2 hrs.   Date:___________
(round trip)

A staff favorite starting at the Backcountry Trailhead, this route links several trails before climbing onto the Edwards Plateau. The hike finishes at a limestone bluff with sweeping views of Government Canyon.

Trail Notes: _______________________________________________

_______________________________________________

_______________________________________________

☐ **JOE JOHNSTON ROUTE**  5.7 mi. •  Moderate – • 3 – 5 hrs.   Date:___________
(Zizelmann House and back)  (round trip)  Challenging

Starting at the Backcountry Trailhead, this out-and-back route leads to the historic Zizelmann House and showcases changing vegetation as you head north. Summer heat can make this hike demanding, so bring plenty of water, use sun protection, and take your time.

Trail Notes: _______________________________________________

_______________________________________________

_______________________________________________

☐ **WILDCAT CANYON Trail**     1.64 mi. •  Challenging  • 1 –1.5 hrs.   Date:___________

This rugged trail passes beneath forest canopy, across limestone outcrops, and along the edge of the Balcones Escarpment.

Trail Notes: _______________________________________________

_______________________________________________

_______________________________________________

# Government Canyon State Natural Area

☐ **SENDERO BALCONES LOOP**   4.48 mi. • Challenging • 1 – 1.5 hrs.   Date:__________

This challenging route winds through wooded terrain, crosses exposed limestone, and follows the dramatic edge of the Balcones Escarpment.

Trail Notes: ________________________________________________

________________________________________________

________________________________________________

☐ **FAR REACHES**   2.97 mi. • Challenging • 2 – 2.5 hrs.   Date:__________

This trail highlights the area's unique mix of geology, plant life, history, and scenic viewpoints.

Trail Notes: ________________________________________________

________________________________________________

________________________________________________

☐ **TWIN OAKS TRAIL**   2.61 mi. • Challenging • 2 – 2.5 hrs.   Date:__________

Along this route, the landscape's geology, plant diversity, historic elements, and sweeping views all come together.

Trail Notes: ________________________________________________

________________________________________________

________________________________________________

☐ **THE OUTER LOOP**   11.8 mi. • Challenging • 5 – 7 hrs.   Date:__________
(round trip)

This challenging outer loop offers big rewards but demands preparation. Bring ample water and snacks, especially during summer heat, and use a trail map to stay oriented.

Trail Notes: ________________________________________________

________________________________________________

________________________________________________

☐ **DISCOVERY TRAIL**   1.23 mi.   Date:__________

Trail Notes: ________________________________________________

________________________________________________

☐ **BLUFF SPURS**   1.80 mi.   Date:__________
(hiking only)

Trail Notes: ________________________________________________

________________________________________________

# Government Canyon State Natural Area

☐ **OVERLOOK TRAIL** (hiking only)  1.01 mi.  Date:________

Trail Notes: _______________________________________

_______________________________________

_______________________________________

☐ **CAROLINE'S LOOP**  2.45 mi.  Date:________

Trail Notes: _______________________________________

_______________________________________

_______________________________________

☐ **LITTLE WINDMILL TRAIL**  .56 mi.  Date:________

Trail Notes: _______________________________________

_______________________________________

_______________________________________

☐ **RECHARGE TRAIL**  1.11 mi.  Date:________

Trail Notes: _______________________________________

_______________________________________

_______________________________________

☐ **BLACK HILL LOOP** (hiking only)  4.89 mi.  Date:________

Trail Notes: _______________________________________

_______________________________________

_______________________________________

☐ **CAVE CREEK TRAIL** (hiking only)  1.68 mi.  Date:________

Trail Notes: _______________________________________

_______________________________________

_______________________________________

☐ **LA SUBIDA TRAIL** (hiking only)  .78 mi.  Date:________

Trail Notes: _______________________________________

_______________________________________

_______________________________________

☐ **SENDERO TRAVESERO** (hiking only)  .47 mi.  Date:________

Trail Notes: _______________________________________

_______________________________________

_______________________________________

*Continued on next page*   

# Government Canyon State Natural Area

**Trailward Finds**

- ☐ SAVANNAH RESTORATION AREA
  DATE:

- ☐ DINOSAUR TRACKS
  DATE:

- ☐ WILDCAT CANYON RANCH BUILDINGS
  DATE:

- ☐ ZIZELMANN HOUSE
  DATE:

# Hill Country State Natural Area

☐ MERRICK MILE TRAIL  1.0 mi. • Easy – Moderate • 30 min.  Date:__________

This brief loop near headquarters offers an easy introduction to the natural area, with a gentle rise followed by a descent through native grassland and wildflowers.

Trail Notes: _______________________________________________

_______________________________________________

_______________________________________________


☐ HERITAGE LOOP  1.1 mi. • Easy • 30 min.  Date:__________

Step into the past as this loop passes old mill remains, views of the Bar-O Ranch House, and historic Kitselman fencing before finishing at the Heritage Garden.

Trail Notes: _______________________________________________

_______________________________________________

_______________________________________________


☐ WILDERNESS TRAIL  3.1 mi. • Moderate • 2 hrs.  Date:__________

This relaxed route winds through the center of the natural area, following gentle valleys beneath dramatic peaks and escarpments.

Trail Notes: _______________________________________________

_______________________________________________

_______________________________________________


☐ MADRONE TRAIL  2.1 mi. • Moderate • 1.5 hrs.  Date:__________

Named for the native trees that line the way, this trail leads hikers into some of the natural area's more remote terrain.

Trail Notes: _______________________________________________

_______________________________________________

_______________________________________________


☐ HERMITS TRAIL  1.9 mi. • Moderate • 1.5 hrs.  Date:__________

Popular for reaching backcountry campsites, this canyon route alternates between open sun and shaded groves along the way.

Trail Notes: _______________________________________________

_______________________________________________

_______________________________________________

# Hill Country State Natural Area

☐ **BANDERA CREEK TRAIL**     2.0 mi. • Moderate • 1 hr.     Date:________

This trail follows a winding, seasonal creek and showcases a diverse mix of native plant life. Keep an eye on the ground as you go—animal tracks are often spotted along the route.

Trail Notes: ________________________________________________

________________________________________________

________________________________________________

☐ **PASTURE LOOP**     1.9 mi. • Moderate • 1.5 hrs.     Date:________

This loop circles a former agricultural field, moving through open grasslands and pockets of mature live oak trees. The wide views and shady stretches make for an easygoing, scenic walk.

Trail Notes: ________________________________________________

________________________________________________

________________________________________________

☐ **MEDINA LOOP**     2.6 mi. • Moderate – Challenging • 2 hrs.     Date:________

This rugged trail climbs over limestone outcrops, passes an old goat shed, and finishes at the Comanche Bluff Overlook. Watch the rocky edges for claret cup cactus along the way.

Trail Notes: ________________________________________________

________________________________________________

________________________________________________

☐ **WEST PEAK OVERLOOK TRAIL**     1.2 mi. • Challenging • 1 hr.     Date:________

This steep climb pays off with sweeping views in every direction. A staff favorite, it rewards the effort with some of the park's most impressive scenery.

Trail Notes: ________________________________________________

________________________________________________

________________________________________________

☐ **ICE CREAM HILL TRAIL**     1.5 mi. • Challenging • 1 hr.     Date:________

This backcountry route delivers serious adventure, with steep, rocky climbs that test your endurance. By the time you reach the end, a cool drink will feel well earned.

Trail Notes: ________________________________________________

________________________________________________

________________________________________________

# Hill Country State Natural Area

☐ GOOD LUCK TRAIL     0.6 mi.                    Date:__________

Trail Notes: _________________________________________________

_____________________________________________________________

_____________________________________________________________


☐ SIDE TRACK TRAIL    1.4 mi.                    Date:__________

Trail Notes: _________________________________________________

_____________________________________________________________

_____________________________________________________________


☐ COUGAR CANYON
   OVERLOOK TRAIL      1.5 mi.                    Date:__________

Trail Notes: _________________________________________________

_____________________________________________________________

_____________________________________________________________


☐ VISTA RIDGE TRAIL   2.3 mi.                    Date:__________

Trail Notes: _________________________________________________

_____________________________________________________________

_____________________________________________________________


☐ CREEK BOTTOM
   TRAIL               1.0 mi.                    Date:__________

Trail Notes: _________________________________________________

_____________________________________________________________

_____________________________________________________________


☐ PRAIRIE LOOP        1.3 mi.                    Date:__________

Trail Notes: _________________________________________________

_____________________________________________________________

_____________________________________________________________


☐ BAR-O TRAIL         1.9 mi.                    Date:__________

Trail Notes: _________________________________________________

_____________________________________________________________

_____________________________________________________________


☐ WILDLIFE TRAIL      1.9 mi.                    Date:__________

Trail Notes: _________________________________________________

_____________________________________________________________

_____________________________________________________________

# Hill Country State Natural Area

- [ ] **SPRING BRANCH TRAIL** — 6.4 mi. — Date:_________

  Trail Notes: _______________________________________________
  _______________________________________________
  _______________________________________________

- [ ] **CHAQUITA FALLS TRAIL** — 0.3 mi. — Date:_________

  Trail Notes: _______________________________________________
  _______________________________________________
  _______________________________________________

- [ ] **CEDAR LOOP** — 1.4 mi. — Date:_________

  Trail Notes: _______________________________________________
  _______________________________________________
  _______________________________________________

- [ ] **EAGLE LOOP** — 1.4 mi. — Date:_________

  Trail Notes: _______________________________________________
  _______________________________________________
  _______________________________________________

## 📍 Trailward Finds

- [ ] **SCENIC OVERLOOK**
  DATE:
- [ ] **HISTORIC SPRING BARN**
  DATE:
- [ ] **HERITAGE GARDEN**
  DATE:
- [ ] **COMANCHE BLUFF**
  DATE:

**Park Website**    **Trail Map**

Visit the Texas Parks & Wildlife
Department at tpwd.texas.gov

# Honey Creek State Natural Area

This park is only accessible through guided tours.
Use this page to document trail names, mileage, time, and difficulty on your tour. No **Trail Map** avalible for this park.

☐ • • Date:___________

Trail Notes: _______________________________________________

_______________________________________________

_______________________________________________

_______________________________________________

☐ • • Date:___________

Trail Notes: _______________________________________________

_______________________________________________

_______________________________________________

_______________________________________________

☐ • • Date:___________

Trail Notes: _______________________________________________

_______________________________________________

_______________________________________________

_______________________________________________

☐ • • Date:___________

Trail Notes: _______________________________________________

_______________________________________________

_______________________________________________

_______________________________________________

## 📍 Trailward Finds

☐ DATE:

☐ DATE:

☐ DATE:

☐ DATE:

☐ DATE:

### Park Website

Visit the Texas Parks & Wildlife
Department at tpwd.texas.gov

# Hueco Tanks State Historic Site

☐ **NORTH MOUNTAIN TRAIL**     0.7 mi. (one way)   •   Easy   •   45 min.   Date:_________

Start out on the Picnic Area Trail and make your way toward the towering cliffs of North Mountain. The dramatic rock faces ahead set the stage for an unforgettable hike.

Trail Notes: _______________________________________________

_______________________________________________

_______________________________________________

☐ **LAGUNA PRIETA TRAIL**     0.15 mi. (one way)   •   Easy   •   15 min.   Date:_________

This short, easy walk starts behind the restroom and winds through a small canyon. Desert willows and a seasonal pond create a surprising oasis along the way.

Trail Notes: _______________________________________________

_______________________________________________

_______________________________________________

☐ **NATURE TRAIL**     0.08 mi. (round trip)   •   Easy   •   10 min.   Date:_________

This brief walk loops around the Interpretive Center and leads to an intriguing rock shelter. Along the way, you'll encounter pictographs created by the Jornada Mogollon and Desert Archaic peoples.

Trail Notes: _______________________________________________

_______________________________________________

_______________________________________________

☐ **POND TRAIL**     0.43 mi. (one way)   •   Easy   •   30 min.   Date:_________

Begin at the Interpretive Center and step into a walk through time. This route highlights the park's distinctive geologic formations alongside historic pictographs.

Trail Notes: _______________________________________________

_______________________________________________

_______________________________________________

☐ **SITE 17 TRAIL**     0.13 mi. (one way)   •   Easy to Moderate   •   15 min.   Date:_________

From the Pond Trail, this short and easy path leads to a well-known Mescalero Apache pictograph site. The artwork is partially overlaid with historic graffiti, reflecting layers of human presence over time.

Trail Notes: _______________________________________________

_______________________________________________

_______________________________________________

# Hueco Tanks State Historic Site

☐ SITE 19 TRAIL          0.03 mi. •     Easy     • 10 min.    Date:_________
                         (one way)

Branching off the North Mountain Trail, this short path leads to a hidden rock shelter with prehistoric Jornada Mogollon pictographs. It's an easy, rewarding stroll with a glimpse into the past.

Trail Notes: _________________________________________________

_____________________________________________________________

_____________________________________________________________


☐ PICNIC AREA TRAIL     0.25 mi. •     Easy     • 20 min.    Date:_________
                        (one way)

This short, pet-friendly trail guides you to picnic spots tucked among the rocks. It's an easy walk with a great place to pause and enjoy the surroundings.

Trail Notes: _________________________________________________

_____________________________________________________________

_____________________________________________________________


☐ CHAIN TRAIL           0.14 mi. •   Moderate to  • 45 min.   Date:_________
                        (one way)     Strenuous

Starting from the Pond Trail, this short but demanding route climbs North Mountain with the help of chains. The effort is rewarded with spectacular views from above.

Trail Notes: _________________________________________________

_____________________________________________________________

_____________________________________________________________


☐ CUEVA DE LEÓN          0.1 mi.                            Date:_________
  TRAIL

Trail Notes: _________________________________________________

_____________________________________________________________

_____________________________________________________________


Continued on next page    

# Hueco Tanks State Historic Site

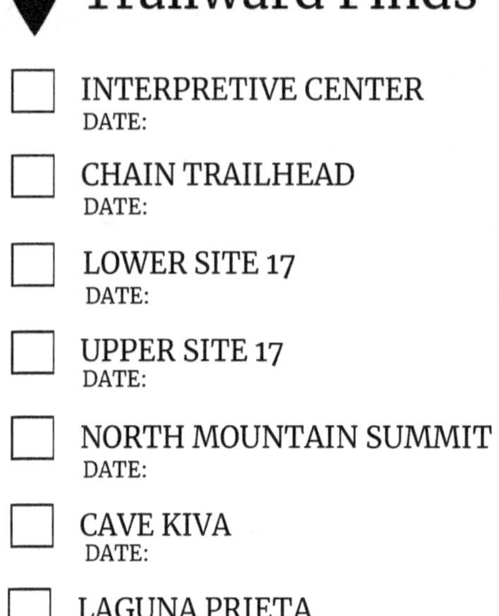

## Trailward Finds

Park Website     Trail Map

Visit the Texas Parks & Wildlife
Department at tpwd.texas.gov

☐ **INTERPRETIVE CENTER**
DATE:

☐ **CHAIN TRAILHEAD**
DATE:

☐ **LOWER SITE 17**
DATE:

☐ **UPPER SITE 17**
DATE:

☐ **NORTH MOUNTAIN SUMMIT**
DATE:

☐ **CAVE KIVA**
DATE:

☐ **LAGUNA PRIETA**
DATE:

# Kickapoo Cavern State Park

☐ **SEARGEANT MEMORIAL TRAIL** — 0.7 mi. • Moderate — Date:__________

Starting near the historic sheep dipping pens and windmill in Indigo Creek Campground, this trail climbs about 135 feet to a scenic campground overlook. The steady ascent leads to rewarding views above the creek.

Trail Notes: __________________________________________________

________________________________________________________________

________________________________________________________________

☐ **PINE CANYON LOOP** — 1.9 mi. • Easy — Date:__________

This easy loop connects the Group Camping Area with the Vireo Vista Trail. It's a relaxed route well suited for both hikers and cyclists.

Trail Notes: __________________________________________________

________________________________________________________________

________________________________________________________________

☐ **ARMADILLO LOOKOUT TRAIL** — 0.6 mi. (round trip) • Moderate — Date:__________

Branching off the Vireo Vista Trail, this route climbs about 137 feet to a scenic overlook. A bench at the top offers a perfect spot to pause and take in the views.

Trail Notes: __________________________________________________

________________________________________________________________

________________________________________________________________

☐ **VIREO VISTA TRAIL** — 0.4 mi. • Easy — Date:__________

This easy connector links the Pine Canyon Loop Trail with the Barbado Ridge Trail. It passes through a prime bird-watching area and includes a bit of elevation change along the way.

Trail Notes: __________________________________________________

________________________________________________________________

________________________________________________________________

☐ **BARBADO RIDGE TRAIL** — 2.2 mi. • Moderate to Strenuous — Date:__________

Starting at the Vireo Vista and Barbado Ridge trailheads, this route climbs to the park's highest elevations. From there, it descends toward the Long Way Home Trail with expansive views along the way.

Trail Notes: __________________________________________________

________________________________________________________________

________________________________________________________________

# Kickapoo Cavern State Park

☐ **ARROYO CAMINO**       1.5 mi.  •  Strenuous       Date:_________

This trail climbs from the Pine Canyon Loop over ridgelines into a remote area of the park, connecting to the old ranch entrance road near a dramatic elevation change.

Trail Notes: __________________________________________
____________________________________________________
____________________________________________________

☐ **THE LONG WAY HOME TRAIL**       6.7 mi.  •  Moderate       Date:_________

This long trek north of the campground calls for extra preparation. Bring plenty of water and snacks before setting out.

Trail Notes: __________________________________________
____________________________________________________
____________________________________________________

☐ **STUART BAT CAVE CUT-OFF**       0.6 mi.  •  Easy       Date:_________

This cutoff provides a direct connection between Stuart Bat Cave and the Long Way Home Trail.

Trail Notes: __________________________________________
____________________________________________________
____________________________________________________

☐ **INDIGO CREEK CONNECTIO**       1.8 mi.       Date:_________

Trail Notes: __________________________________________
____________________________________________________
____________________________________________________

## 📍 Trailward Finds

☐ **BIRD BLIND**
DATE:

☐ **ARMADILLO LOOKOUT**
DATE:

☐ **SEARGEANT MEMORIAL TRAILHEAD**
DATE:

☐ **VIREO VISTA/BARBADO RIDGE TRAILHEADS**
DATE:

☐ **STUART BAT CAVE**
DATE:

Park Website       Trail Map

Visit the Texas Parks & Wildlife Department at tpwd.texas.gov

# Lake Colorado City State Park

CACTUS CUT TRAIL   **1 mi.** (one way) • Easy – Moderate      Date:_________

Cactus Cut Trail is an easy-to-moderate, family-friendly walk along the lake's edge. The route passes through cacti and brush with views of Lake Colorado City and educational signs along the way.

Trail Notes: _________________________________________________

_________________________________________________

_________________________________________________

ROADRUNNER LOOP TRAIL   **2.1 mi.** (total loop) • Moderate      Date:_________

Roadrunner Loop Trail offers a moderate hike with a few rugged stretches, so bring plenty of water. Take in lake views from Picnic Overlook, pass the Rock Ridge separating the lake from a hidden pond, and keep an eye out for birds and wildlife that call Lake Colorado City State Park home.

Trail Notes: _________________________________________________

_________________________________________________

_________________________________________________

# Trailward Finds

☐ **HEADQUARTERS AND PARK STORE**
DATE:

☐ **RECREATION HALL**
DATE:

☐ **TRAILHEADS**
DATE:

☐ **ROCK RIDGE**
DATE:

☐ **LAKEVIEW DOCK**
DATE:

☐ **DAY-USE AREA**
DATE:

☐ **PICNIC OVERLOOK**
DATE:

Park Website      Trail Map

Visit the Texas Parks & Wildlife Department at tpwd.texas.gov

# Monahans Sandhills State Park

This state park is all about exploring natural landmarks rather than following designated trails. No **Trail Map** is available.

☐ NATURE TRAIL .25 mi. Date:_________

Trail Notes: ________________________________________________

________________________________________________________________

________________________________________________________________

## Trailward Finds

☐ PUMP JACK PICNIC AREA
DATE:

☐ WILLOW DRAW CAMPING AREA
DATE:

☐ SANDHILLS PICNIC PAVILION
DATE:

☐ SHIN OAK PICNIC AREA
DATE:

☐ EQUESTRIAN AREA
DATE:

☐ DUNAGAN VISITOR CENTER AND HEADQUARTERS
DATE:

Park Website      Park Map

Visit the Texas Parks & Wildlife Department at tpwd.texas.gov

# Old Tunnel State Park

This state park is all about exploring natural landmarks rather than following designated trails. Instead of a traditional trail map, you'll find space to note discoveries

Date:________

Notes: ______________________________________________

______________________________________________

______________________________________________

______________________________________________

Date:________

Notes: ______________________________________________

______________________________________________

______________________________________________

______________________________________________

## Park Website

Visit the Texas Parks & Wildlife
Department at tpwd.texas.gov

# San Angelo State Park
## North Unit

☐ SHADY TRAIL  0.4 mi. (one way) • Easy  Date:_________

Ideal for warm days, this trail winds through shady pecan-lined river bottoms, offering a cooler, more comfortable walk.

Trail Notes: _______________________________________________

_______________________________________________

_______________________________________________

☐ DINOSAUR TRAIL  2.4 mi. (one way) • Moderate  Date:_________

This network of trails separates equestrian and mountain bike use, with hikers welcome on both. The routes lead to fossilized tracks from the Permian Period—left long before the dinosaurs—and offer a solid ride for intermediate mountain bikers.

Trail Notes: _______________________________________________

_______________________________________________

_______________________________________________

☐ RIVER BEND TRAIL SYSTEM  2.9 mi. (one way) • Moderate  Date:_________

This trail system is divided for equestrians and mountain bikers, with hikers welcome on both routes. As the park's longest network, it challenges endurance with a mix of varied terrain.

Trail Notes: _______________________________________________

_______________________________________________

_______________________________________________

☐ FLINTSTONE VILLAGE TRAIL  1.9 mi. (one way) • Moderate  Date:_________

This easygoing trail rolls along to Five Points and Cougar Overlook, offering scenic views and convenient spots to pause and rest.

Trail Notes: _______________________________________________

_______________________________________________

_______________________________________________

☐ SCENIC LOOP  0.4 mi. (one way) • Easy  Date:_________

This short, easy trail weaves through shady trees and leads toward the river for a scenic view at the water's edge.

Trail Notes: _______________________________________________

_______________________________________________

_______________________________________________

# San Angelo State Park
## North Unit

☐ **SLICK ROCK LOOP**  0.5 mi. (one way) • Moderate to Challenging  Date:________

Hike or ride past striking rock formations that a park volunteer says resemble Moab. This area packs a little bit of everything into one memorable stretch of the park.

Trail Notes: ________________________________________________

________________________________________________

________________________________________________

☐ **PLAYGROUND TRAIL**  2.6 mi. (one way) • Challenging  Date:________

True to its name, this trail is full of twists, turns, and ups and downs. It's a fun ride for experienced mountain bikers and an adventurous hike.

Trail Notes: ________________________________________________

________________________________________________

________________________________________________

☐ **GHOST CAMP TRAIL**  1.0 mi. (one way) • Easy  Date:________

This trail winds through an abandoned camp where nature has reclaimed the space. It's a quiet walk that blends history with the slow return of the landscape.

Trail Notes: ________________________________________________

________________________________________________

________________________________________________

☐ **DINOSAUR HOUSE TRAIL**  2.2 mi.  Date:________

Trail Notes: ________________________________________________

________________________________________________

________________________________________________

☐ **BIG HILL TRAIL**  0.7 mi.  Date:________

Trail Notes: ________________________________________________

________________________________________________

________________________________________________

☐ **BADLANDS HORSE TRAIL**  0.7 mi.  Date:________

Trail Notes: ________________________________________________

________________________________________________

________________________________________________

*Continued on next page*  

# San Angelo State Park
## North Unit

☐ BADLANDS TRAIL          0.7 mi.                    Date:___________

Trail Notes: ___________________________________________

_______________________________________________________

_______________________________________________________

☐ RIVER BEND HORSE TRAIL          2.7 mi.                    Date:___________

Trail Notes: ___________________________________________

_______________________________________________________

_______________________________________________________

☐ JAVELINA TRAIL          1.0 mi.                    Date:___________

Trail Notes: ___________________________________________

_______________________________________________________

_______________________________________________________

## ◉ Trailward Finds

☐ **BURKETT TRAILHEAD**
DATE:

☐ **HIGHLAND RANGE OVERLOOK**
DATE:

☐ **ARMADILLO RIDGE**
DATE:

☐ **BELL'S POINT**
DATE:

☐ **FIVE POINTS**
DATE:

☐ **COUGAR OVERLOOK**
DATE:

☐ **GHOST CAMP**
DATE:

☐ **BELL'S TRAILHEAD**
DATE:

☐ **PERMIAN TRACK SITE**
DATE:

Park Website          Trail Map

Visit the Texas Parks & Wildlife
Department at tpwd.texas.gov

# San Angelo State Park
## South Unit

☐ ROADRUNNER LOOP — 3.0 mi. (round trip) • Easy — Date:________

This easy hiking-only loop near the campground passes a birdwatching blind and overlooks areas where bison and longhorns are often seen.

Trail Notes: ______________________________________________________________________

___________________________________________________________________________________

___________________________________________________________________________________

☐ RED DAM LOOP — 0.8 mi. (one way) • Moderate — Date:________

This trail crosses an old lakebed and climbs to the top of a historic earthen dam. From the crest, enjoy views of O.C. Fisher Lake and the surrounding rolling plains.

Trail Notes: ______________________________________________________________________

___________________________________________________________________________________

___________________________________________________________________________________

☐ TALLEY VALLEY TRAIL — 0.6 mi. (one way) • Moderate — Date:________

Popular with hikers and bikers, this trail drops from ridgetops into lush valley bottoms. Access it from the Red Arroyo Trailhead via the Chaparral or Horny Toad routes.

Trail Notes: ______________________________________________________________________

___________________________________________________________________________________

___________________________________________________________________________________

☐ TASAJILLO FLATS TRAIL — 1.5 mi. (one way) • Moderate — Date:________

The path curves through dense cedar trees, offering chances to spot armadillos foraging along the forest floor.

Trail Notes: ______________________________________________________________________

___________________________________________________________________________________

___________________________________________________________________________________

☐ WINDING SNAKE TRAIL — 1.6 mi. (one way) • Moderate — Date:________

This is a popular trail for beginning and intermediate mountain bikers.

Trail Notes: ______________________________________________________________________

___________________________________________________________________________________

___________________________________________________________________________________

# San Angelo State Park
## South Unit

☐ **ROLLER COASTER TRAIL**  1.0 mi. (one way)  •  Challenging  Date:________

True to its name, this twisting trail packs plenty of ups and downs. It's a bold ride for mountain bikers and a challenging hike on foot.

Trail Notes: _______________________________________________

_______________________________________________

_______________________________________________

☐ **POTT'S CREEK LOOP**  1.8 mi. (one way)  •  Moderate  Date:________

This route winds through a creek bed before climbing to the top of Armadillo Ridge. The payoff is a wide view across the surrounding landscape.

Trail Notes: _______________________________________________

_______________________________________________

_______________________________________________

☐ **HORNY TOAD TRAIL**  2.0 mi.  Date:________

Trail Notes: _______________________________________________

_______________________________________________

_______________________________________________

☐ **LANKY LACKEY TRAIL**  0.9 mi.  Date:________

Trail Notes: _______________________________________________

_______________________________________________

_______________________________________________

☐ **CHAPARRAL TRAIL**  1.4 mi.  Date:________

Trail Notes: _______________________________________________

_______________________________________________

_______________________________________________

☐ **BURKETT TRAIL**  0.8 mi.  Date:________

Trail Notes: _______________________________________________

_______________________________________________

_______________________________________________

# San Angelo State Park
## South Unit

☐ **PLAYGROUND BYPASS TRAIL**   0.1 mi.   Date:__________

Trail Notes: __________________________________________

______________________________________________________

______________________________________________________

☐ **TURKEY CREEK HORSE TRAIL**   2.0 mi.   Date:__________

Trail Notes: __________________________________________

______________________________________________________

______________________________________________________

☐ **TRAILHEAD ROUTE**   5.1 mi.   Date:__________

Trail Notes: __________________________________________

______________________________________________________

______________________________________________________

☐ **TURKEY CREEK TRAIL**   2.0 mi.   Date:__________

Trail Notes: __________________________________________

______________________________________________________

______________________________________________________

# ⦿ Trailward Finds

☐ **RED ARROYO TRAILHEAD**
DATE:

☐ **BURKETT TRAILHEAD**
DATE:

☐ **BISON & LONGHORN VIEWING AREA**
DATE:

☐ **HIGHLAND RANGE OVERLOOK**
DATE:

☐ **ARMADILLO RIDGE**
DATE:

☐ **BELL'S POINT**
DATE:

☐ **FIVE POINTS**
DATE:

Park Website   Trail Map
Visit the Texas Parks & Wildlife
Department at tpwd.texas.gov

# Seminole Canyon State Park

☐ BIRDING TRAIL — 0.1 mi. • Easy • 15 min. — Date:________

This short hike leads to a must-see bird viewing area. It's a quick walk with a rewarding stop at the end.

Trail Notes: ________________________________________________

_____________________________________________________________

_____________________________________________________________

☐ CANYON RIM TRAIL — 4.9 mi. • Challenging • 3.5 hrs. — Date:________

This challenging hike follows the canyon rims above Seminole Canyon and the Rio Grande corridor. The effort is rewarded with expansive views and dramatic terrain throughout.

Trail Notes: ________________________________________________

_____________________________________________________________

_____________________________________________________________

☐ MIDDLE FORK TRAIL — 1.0 mi. • Moderate • 30 min. — Date:________

This connector links the Rio Grande Trail and Presa Overlook Trail, offering an alternate route to the Panther Cave Overlook.

Trail Notes: ________________________________________________

_____________________________________________________________

_____________________________________________________________

☐ PRESA OVERLOOK TRAIL — 0.6 mi. • Moderate • 1.5 hrs. — Date:________

This former ranch road leads to a scenic overlook above Presa and Seminole canyons.

Trail Notes: ________________________________________________

_____________________________________________________________

_____________________________________________________________

☐ RIO GRANDE TRAIL — 2.3 mi. • Moderate • 3 hrs. — Date:________

Following this old ranch road leads to a scenic overlook at the meeting point of Seminole Canyon and the Rio Grande.

Trail Notes: ________________________________________________

_____________________________________________________________

_____________________________________________________________

# Seminole Canyon State Park

☐ **WINDMILL NATURE TRAIL**     0.5 mi.  •  Moderate  •  30 min.     Date:___________

This short hike starts at the Visitor Center and leads to a historic spring that has provided water for both prehistoric and historic peoples.

Trail Notes: _______________________________________________

_______________________________________________

_______________________________________________

## ◉ Trailward Finds

☐ **MAKER OF PEACE**
DATE:

☐ **SPRING**
DATE:

☐ **RAILROAD BED CROSSING**
DATE:

☐ **BRIDGE TO THE PAST**
DATE:

☐ **PRESA CANYON OVERLOOK**
DATE:

☐ **PANTHER CAVE OVERLOOK**
DATE:

☐ **RIO GRANDE VIEW**
DATE:

Park Website          Trail Map

Visit the Texas Parks & Wildlife
Department at tpwd.texas.gov

# Wyler Aerial Tramway

☐ **DIRECTISSIMO TRAIL**  0.5 mi. (one way)  •  Challenging  Date:_________

This steep half-mile climb gains 775 feet, with benches along the way to pause and enjoy wide views of El Paso before connecting to the Ranger Peak Loop Trail.

Trail Notes: ___________________________________________________

_____________________________________________________________

_____________________________________________________________

☐ **RANGER PEAK LOOP TRAIL**  1.4 mi. (round trip)  •  Moderate to Challenging  Date:_________

Named for the Texas Rangers, this loop circles Ranger Peak and follows the ridge toward the B-36D Bomber Historical Crash Site Overlook, with access to the observation platform.

Trail Notes: ___________________________________________________

_____________________________________________________________

_____________________________________________________________

☐ **THOUSAND STEPS TRAIL**  1.6 mi. (one way)  •  Challenging  Date:_________

Built in the 1930s by the Work Projects Administration, this trail now leads hikers to the B-36D Bomber Historical Crash Site memorial.

Trail Notes: ___________________________________________________

_____________________________________________________________

_____________________________________________________________

## 📍 Trailward Finds

☐ **DIRECTISSIMO TRAIL VIEW POINT #1**
DATE:

☐ **DIRECTISSIMO TRAIL VIEW POINT #2**
DATE:

☐ **CHALET GUARDHOUSE #1**
DATE:

☐ **RANGER PEAK OBSERVATION PLATFORM AND GIFT SHOP**
DATE:

☐ **B-36D BOMBER HISTORICAL CRASH SITE OVERLOOK**
DATE:

☐ **RANGER PEAK LOOP TRAIL VIEW POINT #4**
DATE:

☐ **RANGER PEAK LOOP TRAIL VIEW POINT #3**
DATE:

☐ **CHALET GUARDHOUSE #2**
DATE:

Park Website     Trail Map

Visit the Texas Parks & Wildlife Department at tpwd.texas.gov

# PANHANDLE
### REGION

| TRAILS TO EXPLORE | PARKS INCLUDED |
| --- | --- |
| 57 | 4 |

## — Regional Milestones —

☐ First Park Completed

Trail: _______________

Date: _______________

☐ Final Park Completed

Trail: _______________

Date: _______________

☐ Favorite Trail

Trail: _______________

Date: _______________

☐ Longest Trail Completed

Quitaque Canyon Trail

Date: _______________

☐ Shortest Trail Completed

Trail: _______________

Date: _______________

☐ Most Challenging Trail Completed

Trail: _______________

Date: _______________

## —— All **57** Panhandle Trails Completed ——

152.90 Miles Hiked

Date: _______________          Total Miles Hiked: _______________

# Caprock Canyons State Park

☐ **EAGLE POINT TRAIL**    2.0 mi. • Moderate • 1.5 hrs.    Date:_________

This trail showcases the shift from open plains into canyon terrain, leading to the Natural Bridge. Here, erosion has carved a rock "tunnel" beneath the path.

Trail Notes: _________________________________________________

_________________________________________________________________

_________________________________________________________________

☐ **CANYON RIM TRAIL**    3.0 mi. • Moderate • 2.5 hrs.    Date:_________

Follow the rim above Holmes Creek Canyon before heading into mixed-grass prairie where wildlife thrives. The trail continues along the Caprock escarpment with sweeping canyon views.

Trail Notes: _________________________________________________

_________________________________________________________________

_________________________________________________________________

☐ **OLD RANCH ROAD**    5.9 mi. • Moderate • 4.5 hrs.    Date:_________
(round trip)

Named for the park's ranching roots, this trail winds through canyonland breaks once traveled by cattle and cowboys.

Trail Notes: _________________________________________________

_________________________________________________________________

_________________________________________________________________

☐ **WILD HORSE TRAIL**    2.3 mi. • Moderate • 1.5 hrs.    Date:_________

Ride or hike down into the Little Red River valley and take in dramatic canyon views shaped by wind and water.

Trail Notes: _________________________________________________

_________________________________________________________________

_________________________________________________________________

☐ **LOWER SOUTH PRONG TRAIL**    2.2 mi. • Moderate • 2 hrs.    Date:_________

As you follow the creek through sections of the Little Red River, look for bright white gypsum veins revealed by flowing water.

Trail Notes: _________________________________________________

_________________________________________________________________

_________________________________________________________________

# Caprock Canyons State Park

☐ **LOWER NORTH PRONG TRAIL**    2.9 mi. • Moderate • 2 hrs.    Date:________

Hike or ride this trail along the park's north side for sweeping canyon views and a more remote, back-to-nature experience.

Trail Notes: _______________________________________________

_______________________________________________

_______________________________________________

☐ **MESA TRAIL**    3.1 mi. *(round trip)* • Moderate • 2 hrs.    Date:________

True to its name, this trail loops around a flat-topped hill and climbs to a vantage point with sweeping views across the park's southeast side.

Trail Notes: _______________________________________________

_______________________________________________

_______________________________________________

☐ **NORTH PRONG SPUR**    1.3 mi. • Moderate • 1 hr.    Date:________

This multiuse trail climbs to the "saddle," where primitive campsites and the Haynes Ridge, Upper North Prong, and Lower North Prong trails connect.

Trail Notes: _______________________________________________

_______________________________________________

_______________________________________________

☐ **HAYNES RIDGE OVERLOOK TRAIL**    2.3 mi. • Very Challenging • 2.5 hrs.    Date:________

Climb 600 feet on the park's most popular trail to reach its highest point. The steady ascent rewards you with sweeping views of the Caprock landscape.

Trail Notes: _______________________________________________

_______________________________________________

_______________________________________________

☐ **UPPER SOUTH PRONG TRAIL**    2.6 mi. • Challenging • 2 hrs.    Date:________

Take a walk through deep time past exposed geologic layers and rock fins shaped over millions of years. The route unfolds with dramatic canyon views at every turn.

Trail Notes: _______________________________________________

_______________________________________________

_______________________________________________

*Continued on next page*    

# Caprock Canyons State Park

☐ **UPPER NORTH PRONG TRAIL**  2.0 mi. • Challenging • 2 hrs.  Date:__________

Follow this trail past striking hoodoos shaped by erosion, including the "Last Dance." Continue on to Fern Cave, where maidenhair ferns and natural springs create a hidden oasis.

Trail Notes: _______________________________________________

_______________________________________________

_______________________________________________

☐ **CANYON RIM SPUR TRAIL**  0.6 mi.  Date:__________

Trail Notes: _______________________________________________

_______________________________________________

_______________________________________________

☐ **MESA SPUR TRAIL**  0.5 mi.  Date:__________

Trail Notes: _______________________________________________

_______________________________________________

_______________________________________________

## ⚲ Trailward Finds

☐ **FERN CAVE**
DATE:

☐ **THE LAST DANCE**
DATE:

☐ **THE NATURAL BRIDGE**
DATE:

☐ **FOLSOM HISTORIAL SITE**
DATE:

☐ **THE PRAIRIE**
DATE:

☐ **HONEY FLAT PRAIRIE DOG TOWN**
DATE:

☐ **HOLMES CREEK CANYON**
DATE:

☐ **WILDLIFE VIEWING BLIND**
DATE:

Park Website   Trail Map

Visit the Texas Parks & Wildlife
Department at tpwd.texas.gov

# Caprock Canyons State Park
## Trailway

☐ **QUITAQUE CANYON TRAIL**
(South Plains to Monk's Crossing)

17.5 mi. • Easy • Hikers: 12-15 hrs. Bikers: 1.5-2 hrs. Horseback: 5 hrs. Date:_________

Descend the scenic Caprock Escarpment and pass through one of the last remaining train tunnels in Texas. Visit at summer sunset to watch bats emerge, and find backcountry sites near John Farris Station (MM295) and Clarity Tunnel Eastbound (MM289).

Trail Notes: _______________________________________________

_______________________________________________

_______________________________________________


☐ **LOS LINGOS TRAIL**
(Monk's Crossing to Quitaque Depot)

5.0 mi. • Easy • Hikers: 2-2.5 hrs. Bikers: 30-45 min. Horseback: 1.25 hrs. Date:_________

Look out over the historic "Valley of Tears," once a noted Comanchero trade route, and cross a long train trestle above Los Lingos Creek. Backcountry camping is available near the restrooms at Los Lingos Creek (MM 283).

Trail Notes: _______________________________________________

_______________________________________________

_______________________________________________


☐ **KENT CREEK TRAIL**
(Quitaque East to Turkey Depot)

10.0 mi. • Easy • Hikers: 5-7 hrs. Bikers: 1-1.5 hrs. Horseback: 2.5 hrs. Date:_________

Travel through open farmland once served by the Fort Worth and Denver South Plains Railway, and keep an eye out for wild plum thickets along the way. Backcountry camping is available at Mullin's Rise (MM 275).

Trail Notes: _______________________________________________

_______________________________________________

_______________________________________________


☐ **OXBOW TRAIL**
(Turkey Depot to Tampico Siding)

10.0 mi. • Easy • Hikers: 5-7 hrs. Bikers: 1-1.5 hrs. Horseback: 2.5 hrs. Date:_________

Pass through rural communities that flourished during the peak of the Fort Worth and Denver South Plains Railway era. Take a break at historic Hotel Turkey, with backcountry camping westbound from Tampico Parking (MM259).

Trail Notes: _______________________________________________

_______________________________________________

_______________________________________________

*Continued on next page*   

# Caprock Canyons State Park
## Trailway

☐ **GRUNDY CANYON TRAIL**
(Tampico Siding to Parnell Station)
12.0 mi. • Easy • Hikers: 6.5–9 hrs. Bikers: 1–1.5 hrs. Horseback: 3.5 hrs. Date:________

Heading east, watch the landscape shift from cultivated farmland to red rolling plains. Backcountry camping is available at Parnell Station (MM 247).

Trail Notes: ___________________________________________

________________________________________________________

________________________________________________________

☐ **PLAINS JUNCTION TRAIL**
(Parnell Station to Estelline)
10.0 mi. • Easy • Hikers: 5–7 hrs. Bikers: 1–1.5 hrs. Horseback: 3 hrs. Date:________

Find a cool break beneath a broad canopy of trees where wildlife is often active. Backcountry camping is available at Parnell Station (MM 247).

Trail Notes: ___________________________________________

________________________________________________________

________________________________________________________

# ⚲ Trailward Finds

☐ **CLARITY TUNNEL (MM289)**
DATE:

☐ **CLARITY TUNNEL BAT COLONY**
DATE:

☐ **THE VALLEY OF TEARS**
DATE:

Park Website    Trail Map
Visit the Texas Parks & Wildlife
Department at tpwd.texas.gov

# Copper Breaks State Park

☐ **RIVER RUN TRAIL** (hiking and biking) — 1.4 mi. • Moderate — Date:__________

Wander through peaceful grasslands as this trail links the Bull Canyon Short Loop with the Rocky Ledges Loop.

Trail Notes: _________________________________________________

_____________________________________________________________

_____________________________________________________________

☐ **BULL CANYON SHORT LOOP** (hiking and biking) — 1.0 mi. • Easy — Date:__________

This flat, scenic loop is perfect for families or anyone short on time who still wants a great taste of the park.

Trail Notes: _________________________________________________

_____________________________________________________________

_____________________________________________________________

☐ **CHRIS' LINK** (hiking and biking) — 1.3 mi. • Easy — Date:__________

This level trail showcases rolling plains scenery as it links the Equestrian Trail with the Bull Canyon Loops.

Trail Notes: _________________________________________________

_____________________________________________________________

_____________________________________________________________

☐ **EQUESTRIAN TRAIL** (hiking, biking and equestrian) — 3.8 mi. • Moderate — Date:__________

Watch for wildlife and seasonal wildflowers along this scenic loop that passes through prairie, woodland, and wetland habitats.

Trail Notes: _________________________________________________

_____________________________________________________________

_____________________________________________________________

☐ **JUNIPER RIDGE NATURE TRAIL** (hiking only) — 0.7 mi. • Challenging — Date:__________

Watch your footing on this steep, rocky trail as it climbs to striking overlooks. Stay on the path to help protect the landscape and prevent erosion.

Trail Notes: _________________________________________________

_____________________________________________________________

_____________________________________________________________

Continued on next page 

# Copper Breaks State Park

☐ **ROCKY LEDGES LOOP**   1.1 mi.  •  Challenging          Date:_________
(hiking and biking)

Follow this winding trail as it climbs through rocky outcrops and shaded woodlands.

Trail Notes: ___________________________________________________

_______________________________________________________________

_______________________________________________________________


☐ **THIRSTY HORSE TRAIL** (hiking and biking)   0.3 mi.  •  Easy          Date:_________

This short, scenic trail is perfect for families or a quick park visit. Watch for lizards, roadrunners, wildflowers, and birds near the watering hole.

Trail Notes: ___________________________________________________

_______________________________________________________________

_______________________________________________________________


☐ **POWER LINE TRAIL**   0.8 mi.  •  Moderate          Date:_________
(hiking and biking)

This wide trail is ideal for mountain biking, winding through red rock, juniper, and mesquite. Look for hidden springs along the ledges.

Trail Notes: ___________________________________________________

_______________________________________________________________

_______________________________________________________________


☐ **BULL CANYON HOMESTEADER LOOP**   0.9 mi.  •  Moderate          Date:_________

Short trail into Bull Canyon—watch your step.

Trail Notes: ___________________________________________________

_______________________________________________________________

_______________________________________________________________


☐ **MTB TRAIL**   0.6 mi.          Date:_________

Trail Notes: ___________________________________________________

_______________________________________________________________

_______________________________________________________________

# Copper Breaks State Park

## Trailward Finds

Park Website     Trail Map

Visit the Texas Parks & Wildlife
Department at tpwd.texas.gov

- ☐ JUNIPER RIDGE OVERLOOK
  DATE:

- ☐ PERMIAN SEA TIDE RIPPLES
  DATE:

- ☐ THE VIEW OF COPPER BREAKS
  DATE:

- ☐ PEASE RIVER VALLEY OVERLOOK
  DATE:

- ☐ HISTORIC WINDMILL
  DATE:

- ☐ DARK SKY VIEWING AREA
  DATE:

# Lake Arrowhead State Park

☐ **DRAGONFLY TRAIL**     0.5 mi. •     Easy                          Date:___________

Discover the park's wildlife and native plants on this family-friendly, self-guided nature trail.

Trail Notes: _______________________________________________

_______________________________________________

_______________________________________________

☐ **ONION CREEK TRAIL**   4.4 mi. •     Easy                          Date:___________

Explore shifting landscapes—from prairie to woodland to marsh—on this level trail open to hikers, bikers, and equestrians.

Trail Notes: _______________________________________________

_______________________________________________

_______________________________________________

☐ **MESQUITE RIDGE TRAIL**     0.6 mi. •  Moderate                     Date:___________

Hike or bike this scenic connector from Onion Creek Trail to the campgrounds, stopping at an expansive overlook along the way.

Trail Notes: _______________________________________________

_______________________________________________

_______________________________________________

## 📍 Trailward Finds

☐ **WILD PLUM THICKET**
DATE:

☐ **HIGH WATER CROSSING**
DATE:

☐ **DISC GOLF COURSE**
DATE:

☐ **MESQUITE RIDGE OVERLOOK**
DATE:

☐ **"THE HORN" TUNNEL**
DATE:

☐ **SANDSTONE OUTCROP**
DATE:

☐ **WATERFOWL VIEWING**
DATE:

☐ **SPILLWAY OVERLOOK**
DATE:

☐ **OIL WELL PUMPJACK**
DATE:

Park Website          Trail Map

Visit the Texas Parks & Wildlife
Department at tpwd.texas.gov

# Palo Duro Canyon State Park

☐ CCC TRAIL    1.4 mi. (one way) • Difficult • 1.5 hr.    Date:__________

Cross four historic CCC bridges as you descend 500 feet from the canyon rim to the floor, passing through four distinct geologic layers.

Trail Notes: _______________________________________________

_______________________________________________

_______________________________________________

☐ CAPITOL PEAK TRAIL    3.5 mi. (loop) • Easy to Difficult • 1.5 hrs.    Date:__________

This mountain biking trail loops through scenic canyon country around Capitol Peak, offering Green (easy), Blue (moderate), and Black (difficult) options for a range of skill levels.

Trail Notes: _______________________________________________

_______________________________________________

_______________________________________________

☐ EQUESTRIAN TRAIL    1.6 mi. (one way) • Moderate • 2 hrs.    Date:__________

Ride horseback through canyon country once used as grazing lands for the historic JA Ranch.

Trail Notes: _______________________________________________

_______________________________________________

_______________________________________________

☐ GIVENS, SPICER, LOWRY TRAIL    3.1 mi. (one way) • Difficult • 2.5 hrs.    Date:__________

Named for the dedicated runners who helped build the canyon's trail system, this route delivers a tough workout paired with incredible scenery.

Trail Notes: _______________________________________________

_______________________________________________

_______________________________________________

☐ JUNIPER/CLIFFSIDE TRAIL    2.9 mi. (one way) • Moderate • 2 hrs.    Date:__________

Look for percolation caves etched into the cliff walls—natural formations shaped by flowing water over time.

Trail Notes: _______________________________________________

_______________________________________________

_______________________________________________

*Continued on next page*    213

# Palo Duro Canyon State Park

☐ **JUNIPER/RIVERSIDE TRAIL**   1.1 mi. (one way)  •  Moderate  •  1 hr.   Date:_________

Follow this flat riverside trail and keep an eye out for the colorful "Spanish Skirts" rock formations along the way.

Trail Notes: _____________________________________________

_____________________________________________

_____________________________________________

☐ **LIGHTHOUSE TRAIL**   2.8 mi. (one way)  •  Moderate  •  2 hrs.   Date:_________

Follow the park's most popular trail to the iconic Lighthouse rock formation. Bring plenty of water—this route is known for extreme heat, and preparation is essential for both people and pets.

Trail Notes: _____________________________________________

_____________________________________________

_____________________________________________

☐ **PASEO DEL RIO TRAIL**   1.0 mi. (one way)  •  Easy  •  1 hr.   Date:_________

Stroll along the river and pause at the Cowboy Dugout to glimpse how cowboys lived in the 1880s.

Trail Notes: _____________________________________________

_____________________________________________

_____________________________________________

☐ **PIONEER NATURE TRAIL**   0.4 mi. (loop)  •  Easy  •  30 min.   Date:_________

Keep an eye out for Texas horned lizards on this easy, family-friendly loop that winds down to the river and back.

Trail Notes: _____________________________________________

_____________________________________________

_____________________________________________

☐ **ROCK GARDEN TRAIL**   2.4 mi. (one way)  •  Difficult  •  2.5 hrs.   Date:_________

Climb 600 feet from a boulder-strewn canyon floor to the Rylander Fortress Cliff Trail along the rim.

Trail Notes: _____________________________________________

_____________________________________________

_____________________________________________

# Palo Duro Canyon State Park

☐ ROJO GRANDE TRAIL    1.2 mi. • Moderate • 1 hr.    Date:__________
                                (one way)

Wander this shady trail along the canyon floor, passing through the rusty-red Quartermaster geologic formation.

Trail Notes: _______________________________________________

___________________________________________________________

___________________________________________________________

☐ RYLANDER FORTRESS CLIFF TRAIL    3.7 mi. • Easy • 3 hrs.    Date:__________
    (one way)

Hike this easy rimside trail and follow the spur paths to scenic overlooks with sweeping canyon views. Access is available only from the Rock Garden Trail.

Trail Notes: _______________________________________________

___________________________________________________________

___________________________________________________________

☐ SUNFLOWER TRAIL    1.2 mi. • Easy • 1 hr.    Date:__________
    (one way)

About a quarter-mile from the trailhead, look for striking veins of white satin-spar gypsum along this shady, family-friendly route.

Trail Notes: _______________________________________________

___________________________________________________________

___________________________________________________________

☐ UPPER COMANCHE TRAIL    3.3 mi. • Difficult • 3 hrs.    Date:__________
    (one way)

Travel through historic Comanche territory on this scenic multiuse trail. Cross the river that carved the canyon, then climb to a midway viewpoint with sweeping views across the canyon walls.

Trail Notes: _______________________________________________

___________________________________________________________

___________________________________________________________

☐ LOWER COMANCHE TRAIL    4.4 mi. • Difficult • 4 hrs.    Date:__________
    (one way)

Hike beneath the rugged face of Fortress Cliff on this challenging route. Watch for spring-fed streams crossing the path and rest in the shade of Rocky Mountain junipers that give Hard Wood Canyon its name.

Trail Notes: _______________________________________________

___________________________________________________________

___________________________________________________________

*Continued on next page*    215

# Palo Duro Canyon State Park

☐ **COTTONWOOD TRAIL**   1.4 mi. •   Easy   • 1.5 hrs.   Date:_________
(one way)

This easy trail winds through scenic savannah and links to other routes for those wanting a longer adventure.

Trail Notes: ______________________________________________

_________________________________________________________

_________________________________________________________


☐ **KIOWA TRAIL**   1.4 mi. •   Easy   • 1.5 hrs.   Date:_________
(one way)

This easy trail offers views of Triassic Peak, a historic CCC bridge, and the Prairie Dog Town Fork of the Red River. Along the way, get a close look at the 250-million-year-old Permian rock that gives the river its signature red hue.

Trail Notes: ______________________________________________

_________________________________________________________

_________________________________________________________


☐ **TRIASSIC TRAIL**   0.2 mi.   Date:_________
(hiking only)

Trail Notes: ______________________________________________

_________________________________________________________


☐ **GOODNIGHT PEAK SCENIC LOOP** (hiking only)   0.4 mi.   Date:_________

Trail Notes: ______________________________________________

_________________________________________________________


☐ **LITTLE FOX CANYON TRAIL**   1.4 mi.   Date:_________

Trail Notes: ______________________________________________

_________________________________________________________

_________________________________________________________


☐ **SOAPBERRY SPUR**   0.3 mi.   Date:_________

Trail Notes: ______________________________________________

_________________________________________________________

_________________________________________________________

# Palo Duro Canyon State Park

☐ **FRACTURES IN THE ROCK SPUR**     0.3 mi.     Date:__________

Trail Notes: _______________________________________

_______________________________________

_______________________________________

☐ **FORTRESS RIM SPUR**     0.2 mi.     Date:__________

Trail Notes: _______________________________________

_______________________________________

_______________________________________

☐ **TUB SPRINGS DRAW SPUR**     0.5 mi.     Date:__________

Trail Notes: _______________________________________

_______________________________________

_______________________________________

☐ **DUCK POND SPUR**     0.2 mi.     Date:__________

Trail Notes: _______________________________________

_______________________________________

_______________________________________

## 📍 Trailward Finds

☐ **LONGHORN PASTURE**
DATE:

☐ **CCC OVERLOOK AT VISITOR CENTER**
DATE:

☐ **EL CORONADO LODGE**
DATE:

☐ **BRIDGES ON UPPER CCC TRAIL**
DATE:

☐ **CCC FIREPLACE**
DATE:

☐ **WILDLIFE VIEWING BLIND**
DATE:

☐ **DUGOUT**
DATE:

☐ **LIGHTHOUSE**
DATE:

☐ **ROCK GARDEN**
DATE:

☐ **THE BIG CAVE**
DATE:

Park Website     Trail Map

Visit the Texas Parks & Wildlife
Department at tpwd.texas.gov

# GULF COAST

## REGION

**TRAILS TO EXPLORE**
53

**PARKS INCLUDED**
6

## Regional Milestones

☐ First Park Completed

Trail: _______________
Date: _______________

☐ Final Park Completed

Trail: _______________
Date: _______________

☐ Favorite Trail

Trail: _______________
Date: _______________

☐ Longest Trail Completed

Advanced Paddling Trail
Date: _______________

☐ Shortest Trail Completed

Observatory Trail
Date: _______________

☐ Most Challenging Trail Completed

Trail: _______________
Date: _______________

## All 53 Gulf Coast Trails Completed

78.49 Miles Hiked

Date: _______________   Total Miles Hiked: _______________

# Brazos Bend State Park

☐ **BIG CREEK LOOP**    1.7 mi. • Moderate • 1 hr.    Date:__________

This primitive trail follows the creek and leads to the park's northern Loop Trail boundary.

Trail Notes: _______________________________________________

_______________________________________________

_______________________________________________

☐ **ELM LAKE LOOP**    1.7 mi. • Moderate • 1 hr.    Date:__________

This popular route is known for some of the park's best wildlife viewing opportunities.

Trail Notes: _______________________________________________

_______________________________________________

_______________________________________________

☐ **RED BUCKEYE TRAIL**    1.4 mi. • Moderate • 90 min.    Date:__________

Escape the crowds on this quiet woodland trail, where peaceful paths and hidden discoveries await.

Trail Notes: _______________________________________________

_______________________________________________

_______________________________________________

☐ **PILANT SLOUGH TRAIL**    1.2 mi. • Moderate • 1 hr.    Date:__________

Beginning near the Nature Center amphitheater, this trail follows Pilant Slough as it winds through bottomland forest.

Trail Notes: _______________________________________________

_______________________________________________

_______________________________________________

☐ **40 ACRE LAKE TRAIL**    1.2 mi. • Moderate • 1 hr.    Date:__________

This hike offers prime viewing for American alligators while guiding you through a variety of aquatic habitats.

Trail Notes: _______________________________________________

_______________________________________________

_______________________________________________

# Brazos Bend State Park

☐ PRAIRIE TRAIL     1.3 mi.  •  Moderate  •  1 hr.     Date:__________

This short trail leads to an elevated platform overlooking coastal tallgrass prairie and a boardwalk across a seasonal pond.

Trail Notes: _______________________________________________

___________________________________________________________

___________________________________________________________

☐ LIVE OAK TRAIL     1.7 mi.  •  Moderate  • 90 min.   Date:__________

Follow this route along the park's southern edge to explore the rich wetlands ecosystem that defines much of the landscape.

Trail Notes: _______________________________________________

___________________________________________________________

___________________________________________________________

☐ CREEKFIELD LAKE ADA TRAIL     0.5 mi.  •     Easy     • 90 min.   Date:__________

This short, accessible trail offers easy wildlife viewing and features interpretive signs along the way.

Trail Notes: _______________________________________________

___________________________________________________________

___________________________________________________________

☐ HALE LAKE LOOP     1.9 mi.  •  Moderate  •  1 hr.     Date:__________

Explore the park's east side as this trail winds through bottomland forest and circles an oxbow lake known for excellent wildlife viewing.

Trail Notes: _______________________________________________

___________________________________________________________

___________________________________________________________

☐ HORSESHOE LAKE LOOP     1.3 mi.                 Date:__________

Trail Notes: _______________________________________________

___________________________________________________________

___________________________________________________________

☐ HOOT'S HOLLOW TRAIL     0.5 mi.                 Date:__________

Trail Notes: _______________________________________________

___________________________________________________________

___________________________________________________________

# Brazos Bend State Park

☐ SPILLWAY TRAIL          0.6 mi.                    Date:___________

Trail Notes: ____________________________________________
________________________________________________________
________________________________________________________

☐ LIVE OAK TRAIL          1.7 mi.                    Date:___________

Trail Notes: ____________________________________________
________________________________________________________
________________________________________________________

☐ CREEKWOOD LAKE
   TRAIL - LONG            3.3 mi.                    Date:___________

Trail Notes: ____________________________________________
________________________________________________________
________________________________________________________

☐ CREEKWOOD LAKE
   TRAIL - SHORT           2.7 mi.                    Date:___________

Trail Notes: ____________________________________________
________________________________________________________
________________________________________________________

☐ CREEKFIELD LAKE
   WOODLAND TRAIL          0.6 mi.                    Date:___________

Trail Notes: ____________________________________________
________________________________________________________
________________________________________________________

☐ OBSERVATORY TRAIL  0.03 mi.                        Date:___________
   (hiking only)

Trail Notes: ____________________________________________
________________________________________________________
________________________________________________________

☐ CAMPGROUND TRAIL  0.3 mi.                          Date:___________

Trail Notes: ____________________________________________
________________________________________________________
________________________________________________________

# Brazos Bend State Park

☐ **BIG CREEK BRIDGE TRAIL**     0.5 mi.                    Date:__________

Trail Notes: ______________________________________

______________________________________

______________________________________

☐ **BAYOU TRAIL**     1.4 mi.                    Date:__________

Trail Notes: ______________________________________

______________________________________

______________________________________

☐ **HALE LAKE WOODLAND TRAIL**     0.4 mi.                    Date:__________

Trail Notes: ______________________________________

______________________________________

______________________________________

☐ **SAWMILL TRAIL**     1.8 mi.                    Date:__________

Trail Notes: ______________________________________

______________________________________

______________________________________

☐ **BLUESTEM TRAIL**     1.0 mi.                    Date:__________

Trail Notes: ______________________________________

______________________________________

______________________________________

☐ **WHITE OAK TRAIL**     1.7 mi.                    Date:__________

Trail Notes: ______________________________________

______________________________________

______________________________________

☐ **FRANKY'S DAM TRAIL**     0.5 mi.                    Date:__________

Trail Notes: ______________________________________

______________________________________

______________________________________

Continued on next page   

# Brazos Bend State Park

☐ RIVER VIEW TRAIL       1.8 mi.                Date:__________

Trail Notes: _______________________________________

_______________________________________________

_______________________________________________

☐ YELLOWSTONE
   LANDING TRAIL          0.3 mi.               Date:__________

Trail Notes: _______________________________________

_______________________________________________

_______________________________________________

## Trailward Finds

☐ YELLOWSTONE LANDING
DATE:

☐ OBSERVATORY
DATE:

☐ THE CISTERN AT THE NATURE CENTER
DATE:

☐ ELM LAKE WILDLIFE VIEWING PLATFORM
DATE:

☐ OBSERVATION TOWER AT 40 ACRE LAKE
DATE:

☐ CREEKFIELD LAKE ADA INTERPRETIVE TRAIL
DATE:

☐ PRAIRIE PLATFORM ON PRAIRIE TRAIL
DATE:

Park Website        Trail Map

Visit the Texas Parks & Wildlife
Department at tpwd.texas.gov

# Galveston Island State Park

☐ **ESKIMO CURLEW LOOP** — 0.5 mi. • Easy — Date:_________

Walk this trail to see wetlands restoration efforts up close. Notice how even subtle changes in elevation shape the plant life around you.

Trail Notes: _______________________________________________

_______________________________________________

_______________________________________________

☐ **JENKINS BAYOU PADDLING TRAIL** — 3.3 mi. (round trip) • Moderate — Date:_________

For up-close looks at shore and wading birds, this spot is tough to top.

Trail Notes: _______________________________________________

_______________________________________________

_______________________________________________

☐ **OAK BAYOU PADDLING TRAIL** — 5.4 mi. (round trip) • Challenging — Date:_________

From quiet bayous to open coves, seagrass beds, and restored wetlands, this trail showcases the full range of the park's coastal habitats.

Trail Notes: _______________________________________________

_______________________________________________

_______________________________________________

☐ **DANA COVE PADDLING TRAIL** — 2.8 mi. (round trip) • Moderate — Date:_________

Paddle across open waters where seagrass once blanketed the floor of Galveston Bay.

Trail Notes: _______________________________________________

_______________________________________________

_______________________________________________

☐ **SWALE TRAIL** — 1.3 mi. • Easy — Date:_________

The Swale Trail brings you close to the water impoundments tucked behind the dunes, where diverse plant and animal life thrives between sand and prairie.

Trail Notes: _______________________________________________

_______________________________________________

_______________________________________________

*Continued on next page*  

# Galveston Island State Park

☐ CLAPPER RAIL TRAIL  1.2 mi. • Moderate  Date:__________
(round trip)

This route is ideal for spotting wading birds feeding along the bayous or resting in the trees, including the chicken-like Clapper Rail.

Trail Notes: _______________________________________________

_______________________________________________

_______________________________________________

☐ HERITAGE TRAIL  0.3 mi. • Easy  Date:__________
(round trip)

Short, convenient, and packed with insight, this interpretive trail guides you through another stretch of prairie.

Trail Notes: _______________________________________________

_______________________________________________

_______________________________________________

☐ ALLIGATOR LOOP  1.0 mi. • Easy  Date:__________

Circle one of the park's large freshwater ponds on this trail, and keep watch for alligators—they favor these waters, too.

Trail Notes: _______________________________________________

_______________________________________________

_______________________________________________

☐ PRAIRIE TRAIL  3.3 mi. • Easy  Date:__________
(round trip)

Step into a glimpse of historic Galveston Island as this trail crosses rare prairie remnants on its way to large freshwater ponds. These prairies reflect what once dominated the island's landscape.

Trail Notes: _______________________________________________

_______________________________________________

_______________________________________________

☐ OAK MOTT LOOP  0.4 mi. • Easy  Date:__________

Follow this trail around the oak mott and watch for birds along the way, including the striking Crested Caracara.

Trail Notes: _______________________________________________

_______________________________________________

_______________________________________________

# Galveston Island State Park

☐ JENKINS TRAIL          1.1 mi.   •      Easy                    Date:__________

Choose this tucked-away route for a peaceful look at the park's restored marshes.

Trail Notes: _______________________________________________

_______________________________________________

_______________________________________________

## ⚲ Trailward Finds

☐ COMO LAKE ACCESS POINT
DATE:

☐ OAK BAYOU ACCESS POINT
DATE:

☐ OBSERVATION TOWER
DATE:

☐ JENKINS BAYOU ACCESS POINT
DATE:

☐ DUCK LAKE VIEWING AREA
DATE:

☐ OBSERVATION TOWER
DATE:

☐ ESKIMO CURLEW SCULPTURE
DATE:

Park Website          Trail Map
Visit the Texas Parks & Wildlife
Department at tpwd.texas.gov

"""

# Goose Island State Park

☐ TURKS CAP TRAIL     0.66 mi.          Date:__________

Trail Notes: _______________________________________

___________________________________________________

___________________________________________________

## 📍 Trailward Finds

☐ **FISHING PIER**
DATE:

☐ **NATURE VIEWING**
DATE:

Park Website     Trail Map

Visit the Texas Parks & Wildlife
Department at tpwd.texas.gov

# Powderhorn State Park

This is a NEW Texas State Park that is not yet open.
Use this page to document trail names, mileage, time, and difficulty once maps and trails are released.

☐   •  •   Date:_________

Trail Notes: _________________________________________

__________________________________________________

__________________________________________________

__________________________________________________

☐   •  •   Date:_________

Trail Notes: _________________________________________

__________________________________________________

__________________________________________________

__________________________________________________

☐   •  •   Date:_________

Trail Notes: _________________________________________

__________________________________________________

__________________________________________________

__________________________________________________

☐   •  •   Date:_________

Trail Notes: _________________________________________

__________________________________________________

__________________________________________________

__________________________________________________

## 📍 Trailward Finds

☐ DATE:

☐ DATE:

☐ DATE:

☐ DATE:

☐ DATE:

### Park Website

Visit the Texas Parks & Wildlife
Department at tpwd.texas.gov

# Sea Rim State Park

☐ **ADVANCED PADDLING TRAIL**    **11.7 mi.** (round trip)  •  Challenging  •  4 hrs.    Date:_________

Paddle this route for a solid workout and a guided tour through the park's winding marsh channels.

Trail Notes: _______________________________________________

_______________________________________________

_______________________________________________


☐ **MODERATE PADDLING TRAIL**    **4.7 mi.** (round trip)  •  Moderate  •  2 hrs.    Date:_________

Use this trail to build stamina while starting your journey through the marshes.

Trail Notes: _______________________________________________

_______________________________________________

_______________________________________________


☐ **EASY PADDLING TRAIL**    **1.8 mi.** (round trip)  •  Easy  •  1 hr.    Date:_________

This route offers beginning paddlers a gentle introduction to the calm, quiet waters of the marsh.

Trail Notes: _______________________________________________

_______________________________________________

_______________________________________________


☐ **GAMBUSIA NATURE TRAIL BOARDWALK**    **0.9 mi.** (round trip)  •  Easy  •  20 min.    Date:_________

Named for the Gambusia fish often seen in the water below, this marsh boardwalk is a prime spot for wildlife viewing.

Trail Notes: _______________________________________________

_______________________________________________

_______________________________________________


☐ **DUNE BOARDWALK**    0.1 mi.  •  Easy  •  5 min.    Date:_________

This walkway links the marshes to the beach, where the Gulf stretches wide before you.

Trail Notes: _______________________________________________

_______________________________________________

_______________________________________________

# Sea Rim State Park

## Trailward Finds

- [ ] DUNE MARSH TRANSITION
  DATE:

- [ ] WILDLIFE VIEWING PLATFORM
  DATE:

- [ ] BIRD VIEWING
  DATE:

- [ ] 10-MILE CUT AND TEAL FLATS
  DATE:

- [ ] CRABBING
  DATE:

- [ ] PLATFORM FLATS
  DATE:

Park Website    Trail Map

Visit the Texas Parks & Wildlife
Department at tpwd.texas.gov

# Stephen F. Austin State Park

☐ **BRAZOS BOTTOM TRAIL**   0.5 mi. • Easy • 30 min.   Date:_________

Hike or bike this winding path tracing both current and historic channels of the Brazos River, surrounded by the calm beauty of bottomland forest.

Trail Notes: _______________________________________________

_______________________________________________

_______________________________________________

☐ **COPPERHEAD TRAIL**   0.5 mi. • Easy • 40 min.   Date:_________

The route winds through old-growth forest in a quieter section of the park, providing a peaceful walk where you may notice signs of wildlife such as bobcats and gray foxes.

Trail Notes: _______________________________________________

_______________________________________________

_______________________________________________

☐ **COTTONWOOD TRAIL**   0.7 mi. • Easy • 30 min.   Date:_________

A broad path guides you from the hardwood forest near the amphitheater down to the bottomland forest along the Brazos River.

Trail Notes: _______________________________________________

_______________________________________________

_______________________________________________

☐ **IRONWOOD TRAIL**   1.0 mi. • Easy • 50 min.   Date:_________

Begin near the Nature Center and Bullinger Creek to hike or bike along the park boundary toward the lower floodplain forest.

Trail Notes: _______________________________________________

_______________________________________________

_______________________________________________

☐ **BARRED OWL TRAIL**   0.7 mi. • Easy • 30 min.   Date:_________

From the roadside parking near the tent loop, follow the trail as it winds through a shaded forest with several scenic views of the Brazos River along the way.

Trail Notes: _______________________________________________

_______________________________________________

_______________________________________________

# Stephen F. Austin State Park

☐ OPOSSUM LOOP        0.3 mi.  •    Easy    •  20 min.   Date:____________

Enjoy an easy walk along the path and up the stairs to reach the edge of the
bottomland forest and the historic Brazos River bank.

Trail Notes: _______________________________________________

_______________________________________________________________

_______________________________________________________________

☐ PILEATED TRAIL       0.7 mi.  •    Easy    •  30 min.   Date:____________

Crossing creeks and passing through hardwood forest, Pileated Trail
connects the amphitheater to the Nature Center.

Trail Notes: _______________________________________________

_______________________________________________________________

_______________________________________________________________

☐ NATURE TRAIL        0.1 mi.  •    Easy    •  10 min.   Date:____________

This short connector from the group hall to the shelter loop offers
information about the park's plant life.

Trail Notes: _______________________________________________

_______________________________________________________________

_______________________________________________________________

☐ SYCAMORE TRAIL      0.5 mi.  •    Easy    •  30 min.   Date:____________

Begin near the RV restroom, cross a small meadow, then continue into the
cool shade of tall sycamores and cottonwoods.

Trail Notes: _______________________________________________

_______________________________________________________________

_______________________________________________________________

 Trailward Finds

☐ PICNIC AREA
   DATE:

☐ WILDLIFE VIEWING STATION
   DATE:

☐ OLD BRAZOS RIVER BANK BOTTOMLANDS
   DATE:

Park Website

Trail Map

Visit the Texas Parks & Wildlife
Department at tpwd.texas.gov

# TEXAS STATE PARKS

## STATEWIDE TRAIL COMPLETION

| TRAILS TO EXPLORE | PARKS INCLUDED |
|:---:|:---:|
| 806 | 90 |

## Texas Milestones

☐ First Park Completed

Trail: _______________

Date: _______________

☐ Final Park Completed

Trail: _______________

Date: _______________

☐ Favorite Trail

Trail: _______________

Date: _______________

☐ Longest Trail Completed

Quitaque Canyon Trail

Date: _______________

☐ Shortest Trail Completed

Trail: _______________

Date: _______________

☐ Most Challenging Trail Completed

Trail: _______________

Date: _______________

## All **806** Texas Trails Completed

1,228.01 Miles Hiked

Date: _______________     Total Miles Hiked: _______________

# Alphabetical List of Texas State Parks

# Alphabetical List of Texas State Parks

# Check Out All Our Books in the
# Texas State Parks Series

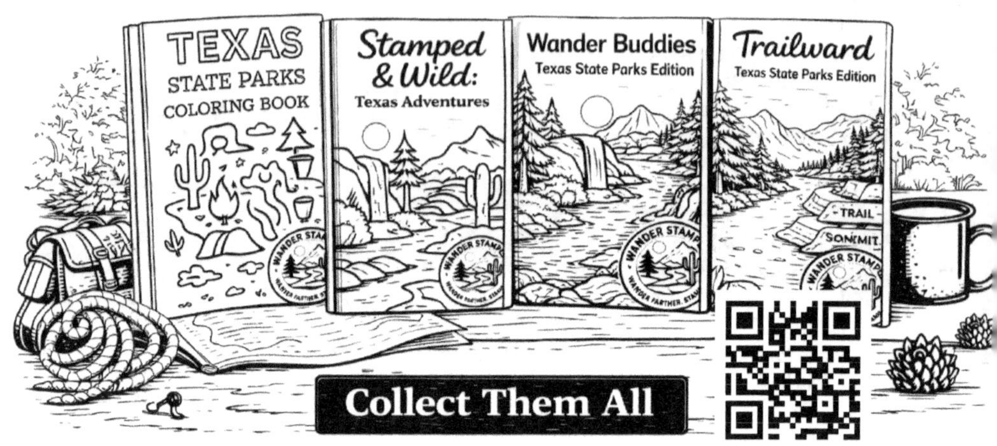


# Coming Soon

# *Stamped & Wild:*

## National Parks Edition

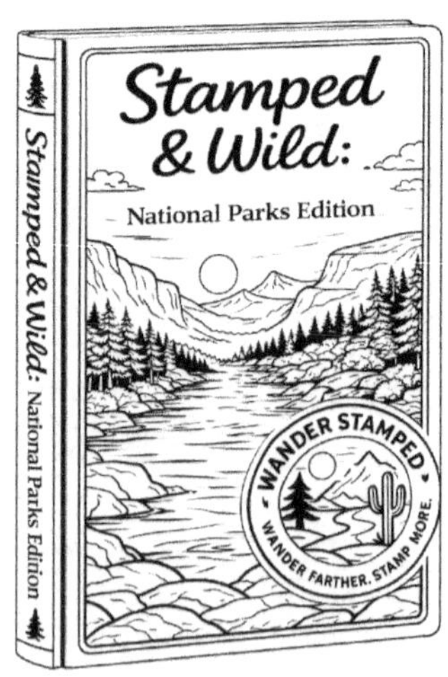

www.ingramcontent.com/pod-product-compliance
Lightning Source LLC
Chambersburg PA
CBHW071502140726
47997CB00005B/1831